LANDMARK COLLECTOR'S LIBRARY

THE LOST HOUSES OF DERBYSHIRE

MAXWELL CRAVEN & MICHAEL STANLEY

Published by

Ashbourne Hall, Cokayne Ave
Ashbourne, Derbyshire DE6 1EJ England
Tel: (01335) 347349 Fax: (01335) 347303
e-mail: landmark@clara.net
web site: www.landmarkpublishing.co.uk

1st edition

ISBN 1 84306 021 3

DEDICATION

Roy G. Hughes, FSA

Printed by Gutenberg Press Ltd, Malta

Design by Ashley Emery & Mark Titterton

Cover captions:
Opposite: Osmaston Manor, 1964
Front: Trusley Manor, 1913
Back Top: Etwall Hall, c. 1904
Back Bottom: Etwall Hall, showing the house under demolition, 1955

LANDMARK COLLECTOR'S LIBRARY

THE
LOST HOUSES OF
DERBYSHIRE

MAXWELL CRAVEN & MICHAEL STANLEY

Maxwell Craven & Michael Stanley

Contents

Acknowledgements

The authors stand in debt to a large number of people in the preparation of this book, not least those who helped so generously in various ways towards the various editions of the three editions of *The Derbyshire Country House*, from which this book derives. We would particularly like to acknowledge our publisher, Lindsey Porter, who suggested this book as a way of using up the many illustration for which there was insufficient space in the most recent edition of that work, and to his hard-working colleagues for making such a fine job of the present work.

David Fraser and other former colleagues at Derby Museum have been most kind in allowing us to continue to use images originally borrowed for *The Derbyshire Country House* and we would also like to thank staff at the Derby Local Studies Library, not to mention the County Library Service, especially the branches at Glossop, Buxton, Alfreton and Chesterfield, all of whom have been extremely helpful, not to mention many years of assistance from both the Derbyshire Record Office and former Museum Service. Country Life and the V & A have also been most helpful, but we have not been able to use the images they kindly offered due to the sheer cost involved, a problem which is increasingly making heavily illustrated regional books like this one problematic. The Royal Commission on Historic Monuments, English Heritage and the National Monument Record have been a great help over nearly 20 years.

Heartfelt thanks are also due to: L. F. Cave-Browne-Cave, Mrs. J. H. E. Chichester, David Coke-Steel, Matthew Constantine, Sir Howard Colvin, William Craven, James Darwin, Susan Ellis, the late Sir John Every, Bt., Don Farnsworth, Alan Gifford, John Harvey, Mark Higginson, Betty Hughes, John Legg, Ambrose Moore, the late B. F. J. Pardoe, Lt Colonel TH Pares, Roger Pegg, Frank Rodgers, Geoff Sadler, Edward Saunders, the late Viscount Scarsdale, Sir Reresby Sitwell, Bt., Robert Innes-Smith, Gladwyn Turbutt, Cliff Williams and many others, without whom this book would not have been remotely possible. Others who have kindly made illustrations available are acknowledged with the relevant picture.

Finally our thanks go to our wives, Gill and Carole for forebearance, transport, collation and innumerable other assistance freely given and most warmly appreciated.

We would be most pleased to hear, too, from anyone who can further enlighten us concerning any of the houses mentioned, or others, omitted (usually due to the paucity of illustrations) or are able to offer corrections, for any mistakes are entirely our own, and in a work of this scope, impossible to wholly avoid.

Contents

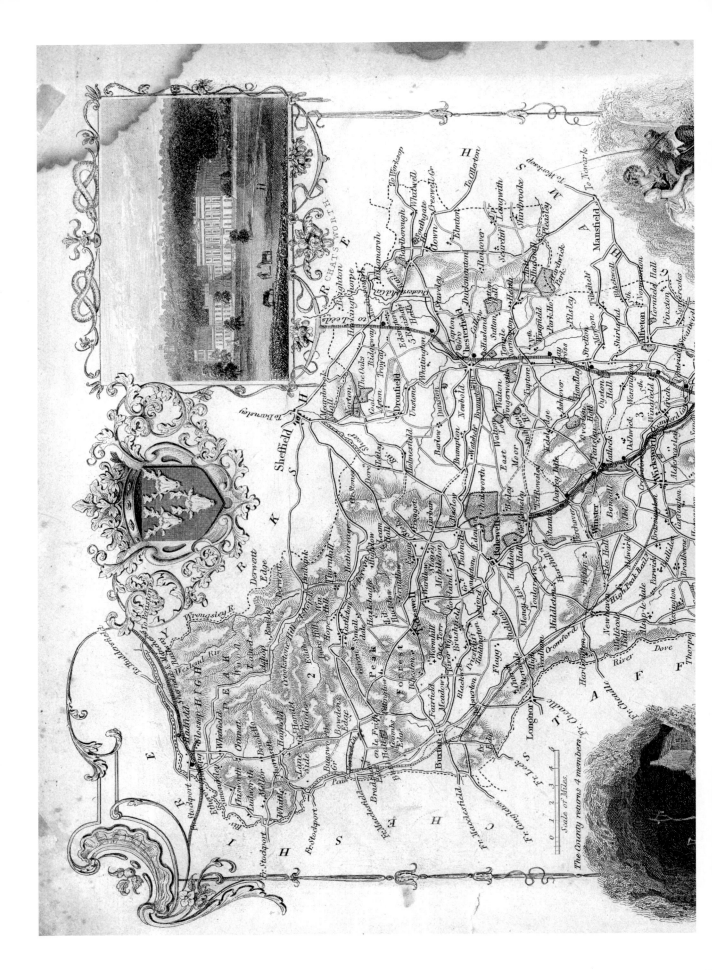

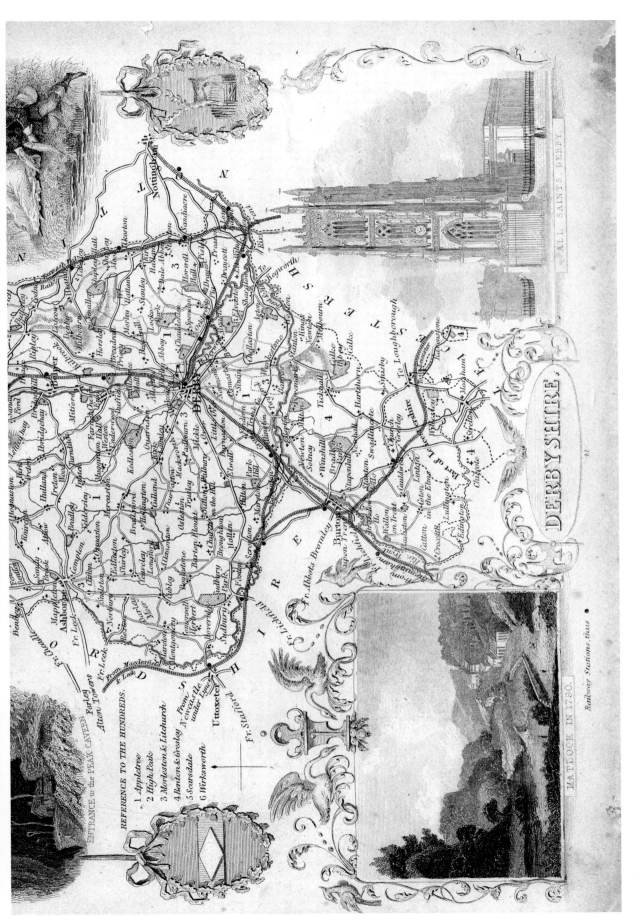

Moule's map of Derbyshire 1845

Introduction

Sir Roy Strong, in his introduction to the catalogue of *The Destruction of the Country House* held at the Victoria and Albert Museum in 1974, wrote of the way that, in the British countryside, we then took for granted our country houses. "Like our parish churches," he wrote, "the country houses seem always to have been there, since time immemorial part of the fabric of our heritage." It would be invidious to add that in 1974 we also took for granted the vicarage, the pub, the shop, the post office and the pleasure of sharing a stirrup cup with the meet on Boxing Day, all institutions if anything more under threat today than the country house!

It was then precisely true of most people that, indeed, they did take country houses for granted and yet, in 2002, none of these simple bucolic things can be relied on to have survived. And so it is for the country house, the large suburban villa and the town house.

Throughout most of the twentieth century, this country has suffered an alarming loss of such buildings, their settings, contents, and the way of life they supported. Their destruction represents one of the greatest losses of our art history - architectural, craftsmanship, fine art, furniture, sculpture, archives – until the 1970s; much of real merit ended up destroyed along with the house. One only has to turn the pages of John Harris's entertaining memoir *No Voice from the Hall: Early Memories of a Country House Snooper* (1998) to realise that it was not just the fabric of the houses that was lost for ever, but innumerable minor (and some major) treasures mouldered away in situ, were stolen, vandalised or merely trashed.

There are still those among us who see all this as part of the passing of an outmoded, over-privileged order, heralding a new age of equality, social "progress" and opportunity for all, the ripping down of the perceived shibboleths of class, of hierarchy, and of oppression. Yet the country house provided jobs in isolated rural communities where few alternatives were to hand, incentives to high agricultural productivity, security, and revenue for the treasury. The communities that revolved around them also gave opportunity for betterment to countless individuals from humble backgrounds, and those who were responsible for their continuance provided constant patronage to that end. One only has to look at the careers of men like Sir Joseph Paxton under the patronage of the "Bachelor" Duke of Devonshire to realize that they were only the more prominent of a constant stream of talent brought on by the way of life which revolved around our country houses.

Derided today as "paternalism", such largely benevolent attitudes remain to many people infinitely preferable to the gauche and unpredictable patronage of the state today, with its inflexible rules and petty bureaucracy. That there were on occasion desperate times and unfeeling landlords cannot be denied, even setting aside the exceptional cases of parts of Ireland and highland Scotland in the 19th century, but much recent research (and the knowledge of those of us who grew up in such an ambience) has convincingly demonstrated that the vast majority of landowners were benevolent both in intent and in practice.

Human nature inevitably tends towards competitiveness, and the history of the imposition by bloody force of ideologies during the last century has convincingly demonstrated that whatever convictions and revolutionary theories abound, hierarchies will always quickly evolve, the one rapidly superseding the other. Some group always ends up in the driving seat, to shower favours and economic benefits upon its supporters and followers. Those that evolve slowly and change imperceptibly hurt the least and tend to benefit the most. And while change is inevitable, rapid change invariably causes more damage to lives, environments and property than it can ever be worth.

A serious fault in many commentators, raised under the precepts of these now discredited ideologies (and frequently in academics or polemicists in the ever-expanding media), is to judge the past by the very different standards of the present. As many of such people are what are today referred to as "opinion formers", a good many ordinary citizens have had their outlook coloured by the questionable agenda of a tiny intellectual élite. Middle England, it could be argued, is being brainwashed from the dining tables of Islington, the executive suites of Docklands and the closed world of the newer universities.

Thus it is with the country houses of Britain. They were created by the then ruling class of this country, like everywhere else in Europe, an ancient aristocracy replenished in numbers by service, merit, marriage and commercial success. The process that lay behind the construction of their houses – the outward symbols of their success – involved architects or master masons, and under them craftsmen of fairly humble background, most of them men of quite exceptional talent. These included local men like Robert Bakewell the ironsmith; Isaac Mansfield and Luke Needham the *stuccadores*; Samuel Watson, Elias Hall, Richard Brown and Henri Nadauld, carvers; Aeneas Evans, Samuel Brown, Richard Booth and Thomas Cooper, masons and William Trimmer, joiner, to name but a few. Craftsmen like these and many others of greater or lesser renown, put much of themselves into their work, for although paid well by the standards of their time, creativity carries its own satisfaction. It was not so much the sweat of men's brows that created the English country house, but the love and pride in their craft of these numberless and unsung heroes.

These houses were then decorated with paintings, sculpture, superb furniture and other works of art, again the products of people of local, national and international repute. The embellishment they produced gave their patrons settings of sometimes incomparable richness which this more democratic age has enabled the vast majority of people to visit and enjoy. Like all fine things they enrich our lives, whilst the destruction of the houses of the elite, so crowed over by the social iconoclasts, enriched only the property developers, the antique exporters, the art dealers and the scrap merchants.

II

The *Destruction of the Country House* exhibition and its still sought-after catalogue was the brainchild of John Harris, Marcus Binney and Sir Roy Strong, and it turned the tide of public and official opinion firmly against destruction and gave the efforts of many people to conserve and preserve an immense momentum, which produced a change of heart in several levels of administration. Books of the country house proliferated, visits to those that were open shot up, and more were opened to the public. Further exhibitions, like the *Treasures of the Country House* capitalised on this process, and the tide imperceptibly turned, the rate of destruction – running at an all time high in the 1950s and '60s – began to fall.

Another important factor was the *Town & Country Planning Act 1968*, which changed the processes under which destruction could take place. Before that date, the owner of a listed building had only to serve notice of their intention to demolish. From 1st January 1969, owners were required to seek formal listed building consent. Hence Messrs. Littlewoods, in wishing to remove the main portion of the Duke of Devonshire's town house in Cornmarket, Derby, were obliged hurriedly to remove some parapet and roof on the last day of 1968 in order to avoid having to seek consent which they evidently (and rightly) thought they might not get after the 1st of January following [Fig. 1]. The imminence of this Act probably also explains the national peak of country house demolitions in 1968, although there were only two in Derbyshire in that year. Another provision of this timely Act was to introduce spot-listing, which theoretically gave overnight protection to a building under threat. Thus, by the time the V & A exhibition opened, the tide had actually begun to turn. What it did was to awaken public awareness to support the provisions of the Act with sympathetic public opinion.

In Derbyshire in the eighteen years since 1968, only eight houses have been lost, and only one – the shameful saga of Burnaston House – was of major importance. In the same number of years preceding 1968 no less than twenty seven were destroyed. The figures speak for themselves. Derbyshire's worst year – its *annus horribilis* – was actually 1938 (a decade before the Act that provided for a statutory list of buildings of architectural and historic importance) when eight houses fell to the contractor's ball and chain. Thereafter destruction was more evenly spread, 1957 being the second worst year with five serious losses and four in 1964. Taking the post-Great War portion of the last century by decade, in

the 1920s there were 8 losses; in the 1930s, 17, the 1950s, 19 and the 1960s, 20, an accelerating trend. Thereafter, four in the 1970s, two in the 1980s, but one in the 1990s and (so far) one in the first decade of the new millennium. The 1968 Act and the 1974 exhibition together were thus a watershed, and the figures repeat for most lowland counties.

At the same time, the destruction of the first three quarters of the century seems to have taken place in a vacuum. Punitive taxation and a paucity of grant aid and reliefs for owners meant that few could foresee any revival of fortunes for the country house. But with the 1980s, a new surge of unprecedented prosperity suddenly led to a fresh and vigorous demand for country houses, but now supported by fortunes made in banking, financial services, computing, the media, films, music and other wholly new sectors, rather than land. By the first years of the new millennium, country house prices had soared to stratospheric levels undreamt of by the beleaguered landowners of the immediate post-war era. Houses that had been divided or turned into institutions were being brought back into single (or restricted) residential use and new ones were being built on the sites of demolished ones.

Thus, in a single century, the wheel has turned almost full circle, and a new proto-aristocracy of earned and invested wealth has grown up alongside those good few from the old order who were astute (or lucky) enough to survive or adapt and prosper on the tide of new prosperity.

Whether these new families will be able to endure in the same way as their predecessors is yet to be seen. So far, some have shown some significant retreats from the benefits the old order usually chose to bestow on their local communities. Charitable support for the nearby (or, occasionally, wholly owned) village – church, village hall, communal activities – seems not to be so readily given; an obsession with privacy (rare amongst landowners before) has led to greatly diminished access to the revived or new country houses, and electric gates, wire fences, intrusive security lights, diverted rights of way have been reported from all parts of the country. In part this reflects the export from the cities of rising crime and the sheer mobility of the average malefactor, yet there is growing up in some parts of the countryside a new divide that never before existed, partly because this new breed of country-dwellers are from urban backgrounds, often burdened by a whole different set of values.

Furthermore, domestic and horticultural labour-

saving devices have destroyed the opportunities for employment of local people, creating the very problems of which the old order is frequently accused of fostering. In some cases, the second generation will probably mellow and live more comfortably with their good fortune, for many of those now blessed with stratospheric incomes were born into a milieu which hardly prepared them for it. With a new generation, many such people will perhaps live more easily with their changed status, like the vast majority of those in whose footsteps they are treading. There is thus plenty of hope, given the continuance of this new prosperity.

III

Country houses have been destroyed right through the last millennium for a variety of reasons; it is only the vastly accelerated pace of destruction without replenishment coupled with new, often unforeseen, pressures on owners that has so marked the twentieth century; there have always been losses, as this book shows. It also explains why the process has been described here chronologically, rather than, say, alphabetically, topographically or by category of destruction.

The most common reason for the destruction of an important house before 1919 – apart from the random but ever present threat of fire – was usually the desire of the owner to improve the standard of his accommodation, or to expand it, given the demands of large families, especially since the eighteenth century, when people began slowly to improve their life expectancy. In the 19th century, an agricultural boom which lasted throughout the middle years until about 1873, coupled with a superfluity of labour, caused households to expand, and more and better standards of service accommodation were required. Some owners met these needs by enlarging, as with Chatsworth in the late 17th century, or Renishaw in the late 18th [Fig.2], others by demolition and replacement, as with Kedleston – twice within sixty years in the 18th century. In 1516, Markeaton was sold by the poverty-stricken Lords Audley to the upwardly mobile Mundys, who built a new house. That, in its turn was replaced by a new Georgian seat, designed by local mason-turned-architect James Denstone of Derby in 1755, when the Mundys wanted something more modern (although not necessarily larger).

At Calke, two new schemes for replacing the house were prepared, in the 1760s by Joseph Pickford [Fig.3], and in the 1780s by Pickford's former colleague, Thomas Gardner. Had either

Above: [Fig. 2] Renishaw before enlargement, c. 1780

M. Craven

Above: [Fig. 3] Pickford's proposed elevation for Calke Abbey

Sir Howard Colvin

been built, today's Calke would have become a "lost house." Other schemes which did not go ahead included a fine Wyatt-esque one for replacing Netherseal Hall by Revd. Thomas Gresley before 1785. In this case, had it gone ahead, no doubt this book would be looking at two lost houses on the site [Fig.4].

Another factor was the amalgamation of estates. In medieval times, a man with only daughters would divide his property between his sons-in-law rather than leave it to his brother or a cousin. The fortunate son-in-law, if he had an estate of his own (as was almost invariably the case), might have no need for one or more extra country houses, and would therefore drastically reduce one of his houses, abandon it or demolish it entirely. This was a fairly frequent occurrence in the middle ages, leading to the loss of Hough Park, at Hulland, for instance, when the heiress of the Bradbournes married into the Ferrers of Tamworth. A generation later, the Old Hall at Walton-on-Trent was reduced and eventually all but vanished (it is now a garage for two cars) when the Ferrers heiress married into the family of the future Marquesses Townshend [Fig. 5]. Likewise, when Sir Ralph Shirley married the heiress of the Stauntons of Staunton Harold in about 1440, the old moated hall at Shirley was reduced to a farmhouse, in which guise it survives, albeit completely rebuilt.

The creation of peerages also followed this pattern. Earldoms were anciently created by Royal Charter, frequently descendable through heiresses, like Chester, and hereditary baronies came into being through a summons to Parliament. The right to expect such a summons turned them into an hereditary honour, also descendable through heiresses, although where there was more than one it was necessary to apply to the Crown to determine which son-in-law, or descendant, should receive the right of summons to Parliament in the original barony. From the mid-15th century, however, most new creations were being made by letters patent, usually stipulating male primogeniture. This led to the entailment of estates onto the male heir, initially so that they remained with the title holder rather than going out of the family when a particular peer died childless or left only heiresses and the title passed to a brother or nephew. The result was a reduction of redundant houses and an increase in re-buildings.

The earliest losses of houses in this book, therefore, mainly follow this pattern. Many vanished so early that no vestige remains to be illustrated here, like Park House, North Wingfield, an early seat of the Deincourts, and Wynn's Castle, Pinxton. The Deincourts moved to a larger, inherited house in Lincolnshire, and it was abandoned, the last

Below: [Fig. 4] Sir Thomas Gresley's scheme for a new hall at Netherseal, before 1785 copied by John Gresley 1855: the late B. F. J. Pardoe

15

Above: [Fig. 5] The remains of Walton-on-Trent Old Hall – adapted as a double garage, 1983   M. Stanley

vestiges being removed by coal mining in the mid-19th century. Some, however, left traces, such as mounds, mottes or moats – a fashionable adjunct to the country house, which reached their height of popularity in the 14th century – heaps of weed-grown tumbled stone or even bumps in the ground.

A classic case is that of the defended manor house at Pinxton, known as Pinxton Castle, or Wynne's Castle, formerly *Poesfield*. It was built by Ralph le Poer who was granted one quarter of a knight's fee at Normanton and Pinxton by William de Alfreton before c. 1235 and passed through his daughter and ultimate heiress Dionysia, after 1252 (when her brother Ralph was still living, under age) to her husband Robert *fitz* Adam le Wyne "of the Peak" – whose ancestor, Lewin of Unstone was one of the few Domesday sub-tenants to have held land in 1066 and 1086, albeit not the same holding. Robert's grandson, Sir William le Wyne, sold it after 1356 to the de Solneys of Newton, who abandoned it in favour of their equally lost seat at Newton Solney. Pinxton Castle is now represented by a low, motte-like mound on the edge of a council estate and a handful of excavated green glazed roof ridge tiles in Derby Museum.

Bumps in the ground, too, are all that remains of the royal hunting lodge of Ravensdale Park, probably built at the very end of the 12th century, rebuilt in 1315 to include a chapel by Thomas, 2nd Earl of Lancaster and ignored by the Crown from the 15th. It probably resembled that which survives rather better at Clipstone, Notts. Another royal sporting lodge was Beaurepaire (Belper), apparently built by John of Gaunt, sold by the crown to the Leches of Chatsworth and abandoned after the death of Sir Roger Leche in the 15th century; the last vestiges were reported by Davies in 1811.

Likewise, the very substantial moat of Champeyne Park, now lying within the former parkland of demolished Farnah Hall, which was built by the Champeyne family probably in the early 14th century, was abandoned when their heiress married a Bradshaw of Windley in the 15th. Another, much later, example are the moated remains of medieval Brizlincote Hall, abandoned by the recusant and Royalist Merry family after the Civil

16

War through dire poverty. The property was purchased by the Earl of Chesterfield and pulled down, and not so long afterwards the enchanting small existing seat was built for his heir, Philip Dormer Stanhope (later the famous 4th Earl), to replace it. On the other hand, the house – called a castle, but probably a defended residence rather than a strictly military building – which stood within the moat at Bretby and by then abandoned through inheritance, was pulled down by the 1st Lord Chesterfield, because he intended to build himself a grand new seat on a fresh site.

Mention of the Civil War brings us to another reason for demolition or abandonment: war itself. People often think Codnor Castle was "one of the ones that Cromwell knocked about a bit" but it was actually abandoned by the last family to live there, the Zouches. They fell on hard times and migrated to America, and a kinsman lived in a reduced portion before the Neale family bought it, pulled a lot of it down and built a farmhouse from the re-usable materials. In 1643, however, a new house built by Sir George Fulwood, whose family had bought the estate in 1598, was slighted by the followers of the local Parliamentary commander, Sir John Gell of Hopton, Bt, because of its owner's Royalist zeal, and following his death in action in Bradford Dale in 1643, being the house abandoned completely a few decades later leaving only a few ivy-clad walls, all of which have now collapsed.

Not long afterwards Emmanuel Bourne at his newly acquired 15th century tower house in Ashover, Eastwood Hall, in trying to stay neutral, had the place torched by the Royalists in 1643, blown up by the Roundheads three years later and abandoned it for his house in Chesterfield; it is still an enigmatic and romantically situated ruin today. The war also accounted for what was then probably the grandest Derbyshire seat of all, Wingfield Manor, built for Ralph Lord Cromwell in the second quarter of the 15th century and later inherited by the Earls of Shrewsbury, and where Mary, Queen of Scots, was besieged twice (by both sides).

On the latter occasion it was stoutly defended by the Royalists, who were forced into surrender, but not before the house was seriously damaged by the besiegers' ordnance. Once taken, it was slighted further in 1646 to make it impossible to defend, becoming uninhabitable in the process. Nevertheless, when it was granted by its owner, the Duke of Norfolk, to his agent, the algebraist and amateur astronomer Immanuel Halton, he was able to convert the great hall into a perfectly serviceable country house so large was its shell. He purchased it outright in 1678 and it lasted thus until 1774, when one of his descendants decided to abandon it for a more modest new house across the valley, the present Wingfield Hall. Even Swarkestone Manor was damaged and slighted, but was swiftly restored, once the Harpurs had compounded for their estate, only to fall to redundancy in the 18th century.

The one really quirky reason for the loss of a house was that of Bradshaw Hall, Eyam. This brand new seat on the edge of the village was built as the result of a patrimony divided amongst the heiresses of the last Stafford of Eyam, Humphrey. George Bradshaw, not having the Stafford house on his portion, saw fit to build in 1635, but work was suspended during the Civil War. He died in 1646, but work re-started once the Commonwealth had ended. The house was probably almost complete when the family fled the village to avoid the plague. It was never completely finished, and became a decaying curiosity, its roof gradually falling in, dissolving furniture *in situ*, and unhung rolls of tapestry lying amidst burgeoning weeds and nettles. The family ended with an heiress who married into the grand Leicestershire seat of Gopsall (blown up by dynamite in 1951), and the next heiress married into the absentee Smiths of Ecclefechan, so it was not until the family patrimony had passed to the Revd C. E. B. Bowles, a late Victorian antiquary who actually contemplated re-habilitating it, that any interest was taken in it at all. But by then it was far too late, and he sold the remains to the Wrights of Eyam Hall in 1883. Much of what remained collapsed in 1962.

Of the twenty four or so houses demolished or drastically reduced in the 18th century, fifteen – Bearwardcote, Swarkestone, Hough Park, Oldcotes, Stanton-by-Bridge, Knowle Hill, Little Ireton, Staveley, Risley, Renishaw (the Wigfall house), Shirley, Yeldersley Old Hall, Hardwick Old Hall, Morley and Newton Hall – became redundant, either by sale (Bearwardcote, Little Ireton, Staveley, Yeldersley, Renishaw), by amalgamation of estates through inheritance (Swarkestone [Fig. 6], Hough Park, Oldcotes, Stanton-by-Bridge, Risley, Knowle Hill, Morley and Newton) or through whim, as Bess's Old Hardwick which, however, remained in partial use until about 1789 and roofed until about 1870. Ten were replaced: Locko (the fine 17th century chapel by George Eaton of Etwall mercifully surviving), Wingerworth, Radburne, Markeaton, Kedleston (twice), Wingfield Manor, Hassop, Norton, Darley Nether Hall and old Egginton, due to a fire. Bretby was also replaced, but hardly fits either capacity, as Lord Chesterfield was persuaded to demolish by a wily local agent who made a killing from the materials.

17

Above: [Fig. 6] Chimneypiece, said to have been from Swarkestone Manor, now at Calke　　　　　　　　　　　　　　　M. Craven

Swanwick, replaced effectively since the 1770s, was only demolished as redundant in 1812. Others replaced were Middleton Hall, Middleton-by-Youlgreave, Foston (as a result of a fire, as was – ultimately – King's Newton), Langley, Ogston, Stapenhill, Burnaston Old Hall, Thornbridge, The Grove, Darley Dale and Littleover Old Hall. Although redundant however, Grangefield, by 1848 long a farm on the Trusley estate, was in fact replaced by a purpose-built farmhouse [Fig. 7]

But new elements were creeping in. A number of others succumbed to the value of their sites for what we might call re-development. Castlefields, in Derby, was essentially redundant, the Borough family having removed to Chetwynd Park in Shropshire in 1803, but it was still viable as a house and had several tenants up until 1838, when it was acquired and demolished for the building of several streets of artisans' cottages, the developer being the Borough family's agent, who disposed of plots to a number of smaller enterprising builders. Nine years later Durant Hall at Chesterfield was sold and the site used for the town's Infirmary, and two years later the Manor house at Chellaston was sold as old and inconvenient and the site built over. A similar fate overtook the reduced remnant of Crich Manor (on the site of a large medieval house demolished by the early 17th century, if not long before) which was replaced in 1875 by a Dissenting Chapel and houses, as was New Hall, Castleton, in 1890.

One house, Coney Green, in North Wingfield, was destroyed for coal mining, a straw in the wind for the trends of the following century. One other, Repton Park, was ordered to be destroyed in July 1893 by Sir Vauncey Harpur-Crewe, Bt, of Calke, after he fell out with the tenant, his cousin, who rashly objected to his going butterfly-hunting in the park without first having asked.

If one adds the brief interlude between the accession of Edward VII and the end of the Great War, Brailsford Hall was replaced after a fire and Hoon

The new house was only started over thirty years later.

This pattern continued in the nineteenth century, too, with Haslebarrow, Eaton Dovedale, Twyford Old Hall, Grangefield, Holme-by-Newbold, Rowtor and New Hall Castleton all becoming redundant through inheritance, although in the case of Twyford, the inheritance (by the main branch of the Harpur family from a cadet one) had taken place in the 18th century, and its utility as a large farm house only became limited in the later 19th, when it was reduced and the remaining portion, divided as labourers' cottages. Potlock's very ancient manor house was replaced by a smart gentleman's farmhouse early in the century through sale and

[Fig. 7] The earliest known Derbyshire view: Talbotype of Grangefield, before 1848

J. Stretton

19

and Romiley Halls both became redundant and were demolished following sale, one to be replaced by a new, much smaller farm house, and the other to have its service wing – a late medieval structure – converted into a cow house. During the First World War, Allen Hill, long surplus to the requirements of the Woolleys (via an heiress becoming the Wolley-Dods of Edge Hall, Cheshire), was sold for re-development, and houses to serve the rapidly expanding town of Matlock were built over the site.

Thereafter demolitions began to accelerate. Aston Lodge failed to find tenants and the site was sold for speculative re-development in 1919, and a similar fate awaited West House, Chesterfield not long afterwards, along with Brimington Hall, Derwent Bank and Chaddesden Hall. The Wilmots at Chaddesden had lost their immediate heir in the slaughter of the Great War, a familiar story all over the country, resulting in numerous failures of the male line, with resultant sales and, frequently, demolitions. Brimington was in the hands of a coal owning concern, and became surplus to requirements, and a development of the site no doubt made commercial sense, while Derwent Bank, again faced with the lack of an heir, was sold to a medical charity, ostensibly for conversion but, again, the allure of the developer's money was irresistible. These, too, all highlight the difficulty of finding new uses for houses of this type, a problem which lurks in the background throughout the crisis of the twentieth century.

In 1919-20, Sutton Scarsdale was unroofed as redundant, the Arkwrights' local interests having been sold, and the environs of the house increasingly encroached upon by mining and pollution. This proved to be another, uniquely 20th century cause of abandonment, and was a deciding factor behind the sale and demolition of Francis Smith's Wingerworth in 1928, allied to the failure of the male line of the Hunlokes in 1856 followed in rapid succession by those of their heirs, the Shelley-Sidneys and FizClarences. It then came to Sir Philip Perceval, later Hunloke, who failed to find any tenants at all after 1920, probably because of the increasingly grim outlook [Fig. 8]. The setting of F. N. Smith's Wingfield Park had likewise gone downhill, and a lack of heirs, partly through the depredations of war, led to sale to a local

contractor who rapidly reduced it to its service wing and it was sold as a farm. Similarly, Farnah Hall, by then long part of the Kedleston estate, was not required by any member of the Curzon family and failed to attract tenants after the war, despite an unspoilt setting. It was abandoned, shot to pieces by the Home Guard during the World War II and has since all but mouldered away.

A number of larger houses, perceived as white elephants in the 1930s, failed to find occupiers or purchasers, and were demolished, almost all to have their sites re-developed: Cliffe House, Newton Solney, Drakelow, Stapenhill (whose site was at least made into a public park by the Corporation of Burton-upon-Trent) and Errwood Hall, where the family died out and it had passed to cousins rooted in the south. The YHA rented it, but the demands of Stockport for a reservoir in the beautiful Goyt Valley sealed its fate, although the actual site was not, in the event, actually flooded. Osmaston Hall, Derby, was long the property of the Midland Railway (later of the LMS), but was replaced by purpose-built offices elsewhere, and was sold to Derby

Above: [*Fig. 6 Wingerworth Hall, sprigged on a Derbyshire salt-glazed stone-ware beaker, 19th century* *Late R. G. Hughes*

Above: [Fig. 9] Shipley Hall: Cornelia Craven in pensive pose by the Italian fountain, 8th April 1909   M.Craven

Council for re-development as an industrial estate; even the tiny medieval parish church which had started off as the hall's chapel was ultimately destroyed.

One or two 1930s losses were replaced; Culland Hall, no great shakes, was bought by the late Sir Edward Thompson and replaced by a house of considerable merit; Windle Hill, a late timber-framed house of considerable importance and long a farm was replaced by a modern farm-house; Heanor Hall, for forty years the core of the local technical school was replaced by a modern building and Tupton, whose setting had long since become industrialised, was bought by the County Council to form the core of a new school, but burned down not long afterwards.

Taxation was a new threat. It was usually possible to find the money to defray Lloyd George's Death Duties once in a generation, but a succession of deaths within a few years, as arose during the Great War, could spell disaster. Thus Darley House, Netherseal Hall, Bridge Hill and Doveridge Hall were all sold once their tenants had left and the sites profitably built over by local speculators. The same

fate awaited Alvaston Hall near Derby, Newbold House, West Hallam Hall and Rose Hill, Chesterfield, more from the sheer value of their sites than anything.

During the 1940s, Longford Hall was drastically reduced after a fire and Derwent Hall, like Errwood before it and Ford House subsequently, was compulsorily purchased to create a new reservoir, in this case at Ladybower. Another new threat, mining subsidence, led to the loss of magnificent Shipley Hall in 1948 [Fig. 9], Measham Hall in 1959 and most of Alfreton Hall in 1968. Mining expansion also put paid to the continued existence of Sutton Rock, not far from Sutton Scarsdale in 1964 and Denby Old Hall, an important John Smythson-style villa two years later. Gravel extraction, rather than coal, put paid to Potlock House, a pretty small seat on a very ancient site, but ironically, the empty site has still to be quarried, almost twenty years later, an unforgivable solecism.

Crippling economic pressure on owners led to the abandonment of Appleby Hall and Willesley Hall, both latterly in Leicestershire, by their families and, after varying periods of desuetude, both were

21

cleared away in 1952 and 1953 respectively. A similar fate awaited Stretton-en-le-Field in 1949, but in this case a new house was erected on its strange, sequestered site. The demolition of Samuel Wyatt's Egginton Hall stemmed from the same problem, exacerbated by death duties. One house, the eccentric baroque Wheston Hall, near Tideswell, long converted into a farm, with only a third in use, collapsed in a gale in 1952, and a remaining fragment was rather insensitively re-built for use as a farmhouse.

Local authorities were culpably responsible for a considerable number of post-war losses. Derby had philanthropically been left two seats by families lacking direct male heirs: Darley Hall [Fig. 10], an important house by any account, in 1929 and Markeaton at about the same time. In both cases it had been the intention of the donors that they should be available for community use or to give pleasure in other ways and in both cases – in 1962 and 1964 respectively – they were carelessly cleared away, leaving their fine William Emes parks entirely lacking a focal point. Derbyshire County Council, having come by Etwall Hall through a failure of heirs and a lack of tenants, decided to use it as a school, but in the end demolished it first. Others followed: ungainly and improbable Glossop Hall (1957), Riber Castle, unroofed and abandoned by

the County Council in the same year, Green Hall, Belper, a year later to make room to extend a car park, Spondon Hall at the same time to make way for municipal housing (despite having been sold by the heirs of Sir Henry Fowler to the Derbyshire Children's Hospital), Spittal House, Chesterfield went in the 1960s for municipal housing, followed by Aldercar Park (which would have converted perfectly well) in 1962 for a school, Greenhill Hall, Norton, with its late 16th century exterior hiding an earlier timber core, succumbed in 1964 to Shef-field's insatiable appetite for council houses. Breadsall Mount suffered the same fate in 1967, but would have perhaps been spared if the Bishop of Derby, for the first of whom it had been acquired in 1927, hadn't suffered from a bout of guilt and egalitarian zeal and wanted to move to something less grand.

In this post-war period, few replacements were contemplated. Only Stainsby House, large but never elegant, was supplanted in 1973-4 by a thor-oughly modernist house of some size by David Shelley of Nottingham which, like Culland Hall in 1938, probably surpasses its predecessor in merit.

Several other houses were lost to private housing developments, too: Barrow Hall in 1958, a fire victim, Pilsley Old Hall, Netherthorpe Old Hall and Whittington Manor – all ancient houses of

Above: *[Fig. 10] The Hall, Darley Abbey C. 1900*

M. Craven

Above: [Fig. 11] Riber Castle , un-roofed, as a zoo   J. Allsopp

considerable merit – and, as recently as 2001, Willington House. Spondon Old Hall with Little Chester Manor were lost to retail expansion.

Of those redundant in the later period, ugly Victorian Norbury was probably seen as an expensive white elephant, Osmaston Manor – a magnificent and forward-looking house by Stevens for Francis Wright – became redundant by amalgamation of estates, its owners, the Walkers, having inherited Okeover in Staffordshire. The late Sir Iain Walker-Okeover, Bt. wanted to retain the Osmaston estate, couldn't reasonably justify the expense of retaining two quite large houses so close together, and was thus unable to sell the house (which in the climate of the times was probably then unsaleable anyway). Stuffynwood, another Victorian prodigy of no very great beauty, lay empty and latterly reduced for over fifty years before the site was cleared by a corporate owner, and another corporate owner – that of the Ambergate wire works – has allowed the former owner's house, Oak Hurst, to moulder away to the extent that demolition now seems inevitable.

The most recent serious loss has been Burnaston House, a felicitous Soanian exercise in stripped-down classicism by Samuel Brown of Derby from the 1820s. This was allowed by its last owner, who acquired it on the sale of Derby Airport (which had used it as a club house and terminal building) to fall into virtual ruin, bar the inhabited service accommodation. After winning two public enquiries to prevent its demolition, the County Council were happy to encourage a buyer to develop it as a residential home, aided by substantial grant aid from English Heritage. However, with work hardly half completed, the same council accepted an offer from Messrs. Toyota to establish a very large (and, as it turned out, ugly) car manufacturing plant on the site, and the same people who had stoutly defended it then turned round and declared that it "had little merit" and consent was granted for its demolition. Nevertheless, a local developer took a liking to it, won the demolition contract by offering to undertake the work for £1, recorded it, numbered all its stone and other parts, and stored it for re-erection.

Two ironies then supervened: it was sought by a Tokyo golf club for export to Japan, but the economics of the matter rendered the exercise too financially burdensome, even for keen Japanese golfers. It was then proposed for a site in Etwall, but planning permission was refused! Burnaston House (specimens of the interior decoration of which were rescued some time prior to demolition) still awaits a site. Repton Park has been proposed, which is appropriate insofar as that house was given its final form by the same architect, and that the site, as well as Burnaston House itself, were both owned, from 1924 until 1945 by Col. Godfrey Mosley. It would be a felicitous move, if the owner and trustees of the Harpur-Crewe estate were to approve the idea, the only snag being that it would reduce the core estate slightly, but one might have thought that, say, a 150-year lease might satisfy all parties.

IV

The demolition of houses, therefore, can be seen as a continuing process of loss and renewal until the last century, when a host of new factors came into play, losses accelerated alarmingly and little in terms of renewal was on offer. It is this last factor which, until very recently, was most worrying, as a substantial and largely unsung portion of our cultural and artistic heritage was swept away in a holocaust of destruction over some sixty five years, 1919-1974, when 71 out of the county total of 242 lost houses were destroyed, over a third of the total of something like 500 years.

Of the 76 or so losses before 1919, 28 were replaced, but during the subsequent period, during which 168 losses occurred, only three were replaced. However two others, Knowle Hill (for forty years a ruin) and Riber Castle [Fig. 11] (an empty, roofless shell for the same period) have been, or are about to be, to some extent restored. And, of course, Burnaston House continues to exist in limbo.

This book aims to give a visual record of this process as far as the available images permit, and may be viewed as a locally complimentary work to add fine detail to Giles Worsley's *The Lost Houses of Britain* (Aurum Press/Country Life 2002) which contains as an addendum a list of lost Derbyshire Houses which the present work revises. We have concentrated on country houses – all high status dwellings in some degree – for humbler buildings are less well recorded both pictorially and archivally. Some suburban villas bordering Derby and Chesterfield have been included, and a handful of important town houses, the latter mainly the more depleted as a category thanks to urban planning and the difficulty of finding new uses.

Note for Readers

For more detailed information on the majority of the houses recorded herein, readers are referred (by the publication date in brackets at the head of the relevant article) to the 3rd and latest revised edition of *The Derbyshire Country House* (2 Vols., Landmark, 2001) and in some cases, the two previous editions of 1991 and 1982/1984. Where such references are available, the caption will include the (date) of publication of the relevant edition. Where these do not appear, the house will be one that has never before been chronicled by us (headed: No entry). The bibliography will, however, include the sources for these and a selection for further reading. An asterisk beside an entry denotes a revision or new information since the publication of the third edition.

There were, of course, a substantial number of "lost" Derbyshire houses that vanished before they were ever recorded visually, or any images of which were subsequently lost. Whilst probably not complete, a list of 74 such sites (nine of which appear in the present work) and brief notes on each was published in volume II of the first edition of *The Derbyshire Country House* (Matlock, 1984) pp. 84-90.

Many of the houses still standing are protected. The grade of protection is indicated herein by: Grade I (I), Grade II (II), the now obsolete Grade III (III) or Scheduled Ancient Monument (SAM).

Maxwell Craven, Derby
Michael Stanley, Ripon
September 2002

1

Houses destroyed prior to 1700

Champeyne Park, Duffield

M. Craven, 28 August 1983   *No entry*

The substantial moat marks all that remains of this house; it now lies within the former parkland of Farnah Hall (qv). Robert son of Richard de Campania (d. 1236) was of Champeyne Park and Thurlstone, Leicestershire, and the moated house was probably built by his grandson, William. When his son William died c.1350, it passed to his sister's husband Robert Folcher of Osmaston, but was split four ways amongst his daughters, probably leading to the abandonment of the site.

Ravensdale Park, Mugginton

Frank Rodgers, c. 1955   *No entry*

The site of the Royal hunting lodge, probably built in the early years of the 13th century is marked by little more than irregularities in the ground and crop marks. It passed to the Plantagenet Dukes of Lancaster, and thence back to the Crown in the person of Henry IV, and appears to have been abandoned some time in the century following.

A motte-and-bailey castle was built on the site, probably early in the 11th century and therefore by Robert son of Warner de Codnor, *alias* de Morteine. Isolda, daughter of Robert's grandson Robert brought it to Henry de Grey of Rotherfield by marriage about a century later, and the de Greys, later Lords Grey of Codnor (a title now revived in the Leighs) transformed it into a two-courtyard fortified manor house. Their successors, the Zouches, increasingly impecunious, migrated to America and in 1634 it was sold to Richard Neile, Archbishop of York, by whom it was largely dismantled, a much smaller residence being built within the ruins which are listed Grade II.

Derby Museum, c 1956   *(2001)*

This unique and magnificent dovecote, built, like the castle, of Coal Measure Sandstone, was probably of 16th century date. The irregularity in the coarse ashlar shown in the photograph suggests that it underwent a major repair at some early stage. Like the Castle, it was utterly neglected for 230 years before the former National Coal Board managed to obtain permission to destroy it in 1965, a lamentable happenstance.

Cllr. Belfield of Heanor UDC in April 1965 successfully moved a motion addressed to the County Council that it should be saved, but to no effect.

M. Craven, from an engraving in J. J. Briggs's History of Melbourne, *taken from an original 16th century drawing in the PRO* *(2001)*

More a moated Royal Palace than a castle, Melbourne owes its existence to Robert de Holland – executed for treason in 1322 – who was granted a Licence to Crenellate his existing house there in 1311. Peter de Bagworth, a local master mason, was building it in Millstone Grit Sandstone in 1314. In 1416, Jean, Duc de Bourbon, a prince of the French Royal family who had been captured at the Battle of Agincourt, was interned here for 19 years, with others.

The late R. G. Hughes, c.1968 *(2001)*

The castle was always a bit of a white elephant, however, and was "dis-fortified" in 1461. After re-furbishment as a possible prison for Mary, Queen of Scots in 1583, the park was sold to Sir Francis Needham in 1597 and the castle seven years later to Henry Hastings, Earl of Huntingdon, who had demolished it and sold the materials by 1637. The present Castle Farm contains some structural re-mains, and its orchard further (mainly invisible) ves-tiges, as here.

Fulwood's Castle (or Middleton Castle), Middleton-By Youlgreave

M. Craven, from a woodcut in Tilley, J., Old Halls, Manors & Families of Derbyshire (1893)   No entry

Thomas Fulwood (of an old Staffordshire family) inherited part of Middleton through his great-aunt's marriage with John Harthill, and purchased further land including an estate at Hognaston. His grandson, Francis, acquired the site of this house in 1598 and sold it in 1621 to his cousin, Sir George, who is said to have built a stone house – something of a tower house – shortly afterwards and certainly before his death in 1624. Pictured here are the remains as they were in the late 19th century.

F. Rodgers, 1941   No entry

Sir George's son, Christopher (1590-1643), was a zealous royalist during the Civil War and raised a regiment of local miners for the King but was killed in a skirmish in Bradford Dale. His widow sold up the following year. The house was abandoned and largely dismantled in 1720, leaving just a few creeper-covered angles, the last of which – since fallen – is pictured here in 1941.

Eastwood Hall, Ashover (II)

M. Craven, postcard franked 1916   (2001)

Built by the Reresbys of Thrybergh, Yorkshire, as New Hall on their share of the huge manor of Ashover in about 1450, probably on the site of a previous residence. After Prior Overton's Lodgings, Repton, Derbyshire's second lodge-type "High House". Around 1600, Sir Thomas Reresby impoverished himself rebuilding it, being forced to sell in 1623 to Revd. Emmanuel Bourne, Rector of Ashover, whose stubborn impartiality during the Civil War led to the partial destruction of the house in 1646, since which time it has mouldered quietly away, the substantial remains being a testimony to its stout construction.

M. Craven, prospect, after an early 18th century oil painting,
from J. B. Robinson's Derbyshire Gatherings *1868*   *(2001)*

The house was constructed in Ashover Grit and Wingfield Flags 1442-1452 around two courtyards – *de rigeur* for a peer in those days – on the site of at least one former house. The client was Ralph, 4th Lord Cromwell, Lord Treasurer of England. On his death it came to the Talbots, Earls of Shrewsbury, of whom George 6th Earl lodged his charge, Mary, Queen of Scots, there for two periods. On the death of the 7th Earl its park and estate were divided amongst three heiresses, the house coming to the Dukes of Norfolk, under whom it was twice besieged in the Civil War.

The tower formed the main lodgings for the owner and his guests, the state rooms on the topmost floor commanding remarkable views. Like Eastwood Hall, it was really a "high house", but here set within a much more ambitious whole. It was seriously damaged in the second siege of 1646, when one side collapsed.

Gate house and outer wall of the lodging range. To the right can be seen the farm house fashioned out of the outbuildings of the successor residence in 1774. The manor was slighted in 1646 after the second siege, and a portion restored as a seat in the 1660s (see section III). The house is still the centre of a thriving farm.

Dethick Manor (II* & II)

M. Stanley, 1982

(2001)

Peter de Dethick is the first known on the site, around 1170; his great grandson, Sir Geoffrey, added a chapel to the house, by then extant, at least in its earlier phase, in 1245. His descendant, Thomas, was killed in action at the Battle of Shrewsbury in 1403, the Millstone Grit Sandstone house and estate passing to his sister's husband, Thomas Babington. With the attainder and execution of Anthony Babington in 1586 – when there were 42 rooms – all was sold to the Blackwalls and, during the Civil War, to the republican Nathaniel Hallowes, by which time it was abandoned and being quarried by the locals for its stone. Two portions survived to be converted to agricultural use, and the farm is still worked by the Groom family.

Bradshaw Hall, Eyam (II)

M. Stanley, 1982

(2001)

The ancient Eyam estate, long held by the Stafford family, was fragmented amongst heiresses in 1565. The Bradshaw family acquired one portion (not including a house) and in 1635, George Bradshaw resolved to build a new seat, but work was interrupted by the Civil War and his death. His son re-occupied it in 1660, but the family fled to Brampton with the onset of plague in 1665, never to return, leaving the seven-hearth completed section to be converted into a tenement housing "three or four families." Before 1800 a portion of the decayed remains had been converted into a barn, but it had become a complete ruin by 1883, and much of what remained collapsed in 1962.

Brizlincote Hall, Stapenhill (SAM)

M. Craven, 1990 *(2001)*

Built by a branch of the Hortons of Catton who held it from the great Abbey of Burton, dissolved in 1539 when all became the property of William, 1st Lord Paget, KG. In 1546 he obtained a licence to empark and crenellate it, which was "a large stone house, that was set in its moat on a bleak ridge". It was sold in 1560 to John Merry of Barton Blount, from whose descendant the entire estate was seized for his Royalism by Parliament in 1650. The house was abandoned by his son through poverty not long after the Restoration. Lord Chesterfield later acquired the site, razed the remains and later built the present house nearby in 1714.

Osmaston Old Hall, Osmaston-By-Derby

Derby Museum, architects' elevation drawn by C. H. Aslin, CBE 1937 *(2001)*

There appears to have been a capital mansion of the Osmastons here since the 12th century, but it was later abandoned by their successors, the Fulchers and Bradshaws (cf. Champeyne Park). Not long after 1591 the estate was purchased by Robert Wilmot of Chaddesden (chapter 5), whose younger son built the house around 1636. It was quite substantial, being taxed on 20 hearths in 1670. In 1696, Robert Wilmot MP replaced it (see chapter 6) incorporating one range as a service wing. This remaining portion was swept away in 1938 with the newer house.

2
Houses destroyed in the Eighteenth Century

Hough Park (or The Hough), Hulland (SAM)

F. Rodgers, 1941 *(2001)*

Sir Roger of Bradbourne, son of Richard de Bradbourne, purchased this estate some time after 1296 and built a moated house, quite possibly of stone (probably coarse Keuper Sandstone), as Woolley (1712) described Hulland Old Hall as having been "built out of the ruins" of the older house, which was situated close by. Sir Roger's poverty-stricken descendant, William Bradbourne, being childless (although not without male heirs), sold it to his brother-in-law Sir Humphrey Ferrers of Boylestone. By the time his son, Sir John Ferrers of Tamworth, had died, the old house had been abandoned, and clearly became a quarry for local people. Only the dried up moat remains.

Oldcotes, Sutton Scarsdale

RIBA British Architectural Library, Smythson Drawings Collection: elevation of an un-named house, believed to be Oldcotes *(2001)*

The last of Bess of Hardwick's "prodigy houses", Oldcotes was built in ashlared Top Hard Rock, probably to the designs of Robert Smythson, on the site of a previous timber-framed house of the Hardwicks, in 1592-3 for her son, William Cavendish. On his succeeding to Chatsworth in 1608, it was sold to Robert Pierrepont, 1st Earl of Kingston, who later settled it on his youngest son, whose son, Samuel, altered it in 1690. On his death in 1707 it devolved onto the 1st Duke of Kingston, who had it pulled down and a farmhouse built on the site in about 1711.

Locko Hall

The late Capt. P. J. B. Drury-Lowe, from a plan drawn by Thomas Hand, 1716   (2001)

This house was unlikely to have been the first house on the site for John Bird MP was there by 1377. It was built by William Gilbert who bought the estate in 1611. His son added a classical chapel by George Eaton of Etwall in 1670-3, but John Gilbert sold the estate in 1721 to Robert Ferne who replaced it in 1737. The chapel, however, was retained as part of the newer house.

Wingerworth Hall (II)

M. Craven, drawing from a marquetry original of c. 1676]   (2001)

Henry Hunloke, a tenant of the Curzon estate at Wingerworth, purchased the estate in 1582, and built a neat new house quite possibly by Robert Smythson, probably about 1600. It was in ashlared Coal Measures Sandstone, compact and quirky, influenced by the late Elizabethan chivalric revival. Garrisoned for the King in the Civil War, the house was saved on the death of its Royalist owner Sir Henry Hunloke, 1st Bt., by his widow re-marrying a prominent Roundhead. Two large wings (II) were added by 1670 and rebuilt in 1698, but the main house was demolished and replaced in 1725 by a much larger affair (see chapter 5).

Walton Old Hall, Walton-On-Trent

M. Craven, postcard of c. 1906 from an original view of c. 1890   (2001)

Sometime in the later 16th century, the Ferrers of Tamworth built a new house here, their predecessors as owners having been absent since the early 14th century. In the early 18th century, this brick and timber house, at best only in occasional use, passed by marriage through a succession of grand families to 1st Marquess Townshend in 1751. It was vastly reduced under the ownership of the Comptons, Marquesses of Northampton, around 1730, and turned into a farmhouse. In 1875, in local ownership, it became cottages, but was derelict by the 1900s. The remaining fragment housed a motor car in 1983. (See fig. V, in Introduction). The Old Hall is on the right in this photograph and the stableblock is seen converted to houses.

Radburne Hall

Mrs. J. H. E. Chichester, elevation from an estate plan by Thomas Hand, 1711   (2001)

There must have been a seat here since the 11th century, but in the 1350s, Sir John Chandos built a "mighty large howse" here in stone (presumably Keuper Sandstone), which passed to the Poles of Newburgh after his death. It was apparently moated, and its site remains near the church, where a later house of early 17th century date, was built to replace it. This was supplanted on a new site by the present hall in 1739; the old house was abandoned in 1753, "in ruins" in 1802 and was cleared away very soon afterwards when the park was re-landscaped by Emes and Webb.

Swarkestone Manor House

Derby Evening Telegraph, 1946

(2001)

Swarkestone Manor was built on the Fynderne family estate by Chief Justice Sir Richard Harpur shortly after 1558, and seems to have been a house of considerable size, built of Keuper Sandstone ashlar. After the Civil war, during which it withstood a siege of five weeks beginning in December 1642, the senior branch of the family failed in the male line and the estate devolved on to one of the junior branches of this prolific family, that of Calke. When the Countess of Bellamont, widow of the last Harpur there died, it became completely redundant and was pulled down in 1746-48, leaving a number of walls standing, in places to ten feet, some with fireplaces in them and one with a doorcase.

M. Craven, 1993

(2001)

General view of the remains. In 1989 clear traces of the original gardens were discovered during routine agricultural work. They remain sealed beneath the turf.

36

In 1630-1, Sir John Harpur of Swarkestone set about embellishing his house, these works including the exceptionally pretty "Bowl alley howse" called Swarkestone Stand (II*), thought to have been designed by John Smythson and built 1630-32 by Richard Shepherd. This was left in situ after the demolition of the Manor, but empty, windowless and decaying, a state from which it was rescued in 1984 when the Landmark Trust restored it as a holiday home. The nearby Tithe Barn (II), which also survived, was converted into dwellings.

Shipley Hall

Derbyshire County Council, elevation from a diagram of 1631 (2001)

There has been an important house at Shipley since the 13th century, but between 1636 and 1631 Sir Edward Leche of Squerries, Kent built a new, tall, gabled house, later taxed on 11 hearths, which passed in 1713 via his son's ultimate heiress, Hester Miller, to a branch of the Mundys of Markeaton. Edward Mundy pulled down Leche's house, for in 1749 he is known to have had a replacement well under way. The Mundys' house itself later became a casualty (see chapter 7).

Derby Museum, elevation from an estate plan of 1753 (2001)

No image appears to have survived of the seat of the ancient family of Touchet, Lords Audley, but on the sale of the estate to Sir John Mundy in 1516, the old house was pulled down and replaced by a new one in timber on an ashlar ground floor of Keuper Sandstone. A spectacular "High House", it served the family until in 1753-55 a replacement was built (see chapter 9) and it was pulled down. However a new stable block was not provided until c.1772, when Joseph Pickford built anew on the old plinth which, consequently, survives.

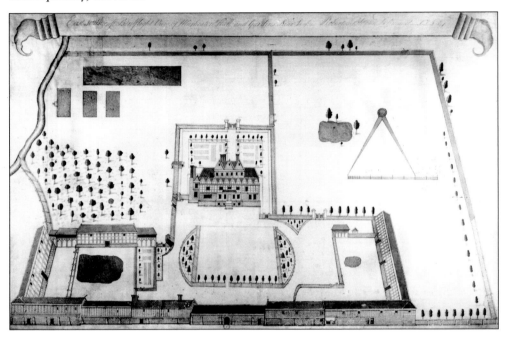

Staveley Hall (II)

M. Craven, the remainder of the E. front in 1862, drawn by Ll. Jewitt for The Reliquary (2001)

Although Staveley Hall still exists, what remains is but a truncated remnant of the house built (on the site of a much more ancient seat) in 1603-4 by Sir Peter Frescheville. It is thought that it was considerably extended by John Smythson after Sir Peter's death in 1634 for his son, John, later 1st Lord Frescheville (of the second creation). He, however, was ruined through adherence to the Royal cause in the Civil War, and left no sons, the estate being sold in 1681 to the future 1st Duke of Devonshire. His younger son lived there, but in 1751, the latter's son died and much of the house was demolished in 1756.

EAST FRONT, 1862.

Smythson's W front was of nine bays, the fenestration being closely similar to that of the Gallery Range at Bolsover. There were canted bays at either end, probably originally topped by low crenellated towers as at Wingerworth (see above). These and another bay were removed, along with the S front in 1843 after a long tenancy by the Gisbornes and the house became a rectory, Sir Gilbert Scott later making an attempt to rationalize what remained. It is now Council Offices.

WEST FRONT AS IT WAS IN 1816.

Risley Hall

M. Craven, Woodcut by J. B. Robinson after a lost 17th century painting, from Derbyshire Gatherings, *1868* (2001)

Risley Hall was a substantial early Tudor mansion built for Thomas Willoughby shortly after 1513, the year his father, Hugh, died. In 1587, the Willoughbys purchased a neighbouring estate and built a hunting lodge on the site of an earlier house, called Risley Lodge, which appears in the right background of the picture. The family's last heiress, Elizabeth, died in 1723, after which the house became redundant. An attempt to sell it failed in 1743, and it was demolished in 1757. The Lodge was to let in 1766, but seems not to have lasted beyond the 1820s, when a new Risley Lodge (qv. chapter 6) was built on a different site.

M. Craven, photograph by Richard Keene, from a glass slide, of c. 1880

(2001)

Vestiges of the Tudor gardens and their embellishments remained well into the 19th century, and to some extent may still do. It is not known if the Tudor house was moated, however, or whether this view of c. 1880 depicts a more formal water feature below the great terrace.

M. Craven, photograph by Richard Keene, from a glass slide, of c. 1880   *(2001)*

A gazebo or possibly a banqueting house, surviving in 1880. The architecture suggests that it is a later 16th century addition, somewhat influenced by Robert Smythson's work for the Willoughby's kinsfolk at Wollaton, nearby.

The mid 18th century was a bad time in Derbyshire for large ancient houses, Morley Hall being demolished and the materials sold in 1757 by Hugh Bateman of Hartington. A moated site nearby probably marks the site of the first house, built by the de Morleys. Their ultimate heirs were the Sacheverells, who built a house later taxed on 16 hearths sometime after they came by the estate around 1480. Thoroton reported that they had "exceedingly enlarged" it by the 1680s. A fragment of the house remains, seen here incorporated into the Bateman Mausoleum by G. F. Bodley (II) in 1897.

M. Craven, 1983   (2001)

One of the Sacheverell heiresses brought the estate to John Osborne of Derby in the earlier 18th century. His heiress married Hugh Bateman, who thereby acquired a second Derby Town house, and the Hall was demolished as redundant. Part of the former stable range also survives, now called the Tithe Barn (II), close to Morley's handsome church. From its Millstone Grit Sandstone construction it would be reasonable to suppose that the house was similarly constructed.

Kedleston Hall

The late Viscount Scarsdale, from a painting of c. 1739 at Kedleston (2001)

Although one of the very grandest houses in Britain, Kedleston Hall was built 1758-1781 at the expense of a very fine brick house built from 1700 and embellished over thirty years to the designs of Francis Smith of Warwick for Sir Nathaniel Curzon 2nd Bt. That in itself also replaced a far more ancient seat, for the family had been there since around 1100. The Smith house fell victim to the sudden accession to power of the Tory Curzons in 1760, after nearly 50 years in the political wilderness, and a huge boost in the coal income from their estates elsewhere. Once the present family wing was complete in about 1760, it came down. At least one of Smith's chimneypieces survives in the present attic rooms.

Foremark Hall

Christies, anonymous painting of c. 1710, identified as old Foremark (2001)

The Burdetts came to Foremark in 1602 as a result of marriage with Jane Franceys, to find the old Franceys seat "nigh ruinous". It was probably then repaired, and after the death of Sir Thomas, 1st Bt., in 1647, his son set about entirely rebuilding it, a process probably complete by 1662, being described as "large and convenient" in 1712, at about the time it was painted. Sir Robert Burdett, 4th Bt. (1716-1797) entirely replaced it in 1759-61, and the family moved temporarily to Knowle Hill (qv.) on the estate. Only the chapel of St. Saviour, also of c. 1662, and the early 18th century stable block survive from this house.

Yeldersley Old Hall (II)

M. Craven, 1991   *(2001)*

In the 16th century Christopher Pegge had acquired Yeldersley from the Vernons, and the site had probably not been lived on since the 15th century. He built a new house, where, later, Catherine Pegge, Charles II's mistress, was born. The house was rebuilt and extended in the early 18th century in brick with dressings of Keuper Sandstone. The estate was sold after 1768, and most of the house demolished, the west range surviving to become a barn until converted into a dwelling in the 1980s. A replacement house was built nearer the main road from around 1800.

Shirley Hall (SAM)

M. Craven, 2000   *(2001)*

The Shirleys, Domesday tenants here, had a substantial, probably timber framed, manor house situated within a moat, seen here. Largely abandoned when the family inherited Staunton Harold (Leics.). This was in c. 1440. In 1789 the "ancient seat" was said to have stood "until a few years ago" but then was "entirely taken down" and "scarcely a vestige" was to be seen.

The date of demolition was around 1770, and a modest brick farmhouse was erected in its place in the 1790s, incorporating small portions of the original fabric, some interior 16th and later 17th century decoration. The Shirleys, now Earls Ferrers, still own land in the parish.

Wingfield Manor (I)

The late R. G. Hughes, great hall range c. 1963

(2001)

The Duke of Norfolk settled his Cumbrian-born agent, Immanuel Halton, FRS on the ruins of the Manor and 1000 acres of former parkland in 1662. He re-habilitated part of the old seat, turning the former great hall into a substantial two storey residence. He was a pioneer algebraist, mathematician and astronomer, encouraging the young John Flamsteed, FRS, and setting up a number of sundials on the old fabric. In 1774, his descendant, Wingfield Halton, abandoned the house for a more convenient new one nearby, leaving only a working farm surrounded by the fast decaying medieval fabric.

Hassop Hall

Trustees of the Chatsworth Settlement, elevation from a 17th century estate map (2001)

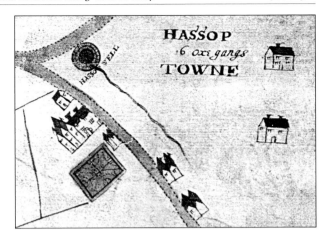

The prolific Eyre family acquired Hassop in the 15th century, and had replaced a previous house by about 1600. This three gabled house, with a lower wing, all probably of Ashover Grit, was itself replaced in about 1774 by a new Classical house. This however, incorporates some elements of its predecessor, including some Smythson-like carved stone decorations, for Thomas son of Rowland Eyre, whose successors styled themselves Earls of Newburgh.

Bretby Hall

M. Craven, engraving by Kip from Le Nouveau Theatre de Grande Bretagne *1715* (2001)

In its day Bretby must have been the greatest and most glorious of the great houses of Derbyshire, if not the entire region. It was built, allegedly to designs by Inigo Jones (there is no documentary evidence for this), in the 1620s for the 1st Earl of Chesterfield. His son made substantial additions (by Le Vau) in 1670, and created gardens and parkland of great grandeur. It replaced Bretby Castle, which had fallen into ruin by 1712, and is now marked by a moat nearby. Yet in 1777 a greedy agent persuaded the 5th Earl to demolish it entirely, a task which took until 1781. The agent made a substantial fortune out of the materials.

It was replaced by the present house (the service range of which survives from its predecessor) from 1812.

Hardwick Old Hall* (I)

English Heritage

(2001)

After her estrangement from her fourth husband, George Talbot, 6th Earl of Shrewsbury, Bess of Hardwick withdrew to her ancestral estate and started to build an ambitious "high house" out of the house her brother had left her. Work went on using Coal Measure Sandstone from 1587 until 1591, by which time Lord Shrewsbury had died, and she began building the present Hardwick, which contains less accommodation than one might

expect, the Old Hall acting, like the Gallery Range at Bolsover, as a detached guest wing. This late 17th century view shows the house when still intact.

M. Craven, albumen print detached from an album (2001)

Once Chatsworth had been rebuilt, Hardwick, now out of fashion, was rarely used. The east wing was unroofed in 1746, although the rest of the house was not fully abandoned until 1789, when the kitchens, housekeeper's suite (which included the impressively stuccoed Hill Great chamber) and staff dormitories finally went out of use. The central section was then dismantled, but the west wing remained covered until the 1870s, as here, photographed by Richard Keene of Derby c. 1871.

Bearwardcote Hall

D. Farnsworth, moat and bridge, 1984

(2001)

In 1658 the Bonington family had a "good house moted round with a bridge of stone and a gatehouse", by then probably quite ancient. They were forced to sell in 1674 to William Turner, their Derby attorney, through poverty, and his descendant Exuperius Turner sold it to the Newtons of Mickleover in 1790, who immediately demolished it, a replacement not being provided until 1886. The moat and stone bridge of Keuper Sandstone survive, hidden in undergrowth.

Norton Hall

M. Craven, from an 18th century engraving, copied from a much earlier painting (2001)

The original house, which from appearances might have been a Smythson-influenced tower house akin to Tupton (see chapter 6), was built in Coal Measure Sandstone after 1622 by John Bullock of Unstone. He bought the estate of the Blythes, who had had a previous house here from the late 15th century. From 1664 it included a Presbyterian chapel. In c. 1710-20 it was radically rebuilt by the Offleys, but demolished and replaced in 1793 by Samuel Shore, their heir.

Darley Nether Hall, Darley Dale

M. Craven, re-drawn from an original in the Woolley MSS in the British Library No entry

There were two halls at Darley, one, built by the Columbells, had become ruinous not long after 1670 and was cleared by the Duke of Rutland in 1776. Nether Hall at Churchtown, however, was the seat of the de Darleys, and was built c. 1321. It passed through many ownerships after being sold by the Foljambes and was long tenanted. It finally came into the hands of Sir Richard Arkwright from the Wrays, impoverished baronets, and was pulled down by him in 1796, although some portions of standing decorative stonework survived near the Square and Compasses Inn until after the 1840s.

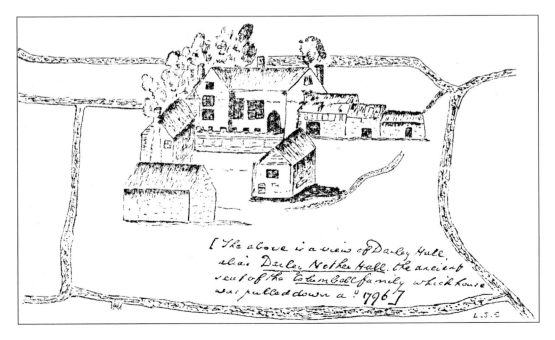

[The above is a view of Darley Hall alias Darley Nether Hall, the ancient seat of the Columbell family which house was pulled down a⁰ 1796]

3
Nineteenth Century Losses

Old St. Helen's House, Derby

M. Craven, engraving by Orlando Jewitt after a painting by Sir William Gell, 1792   *No entry*

The Augustinian convent of St. Helen was founded c. 1137 and, at the Dissolution, became a Foljambe family residence. By the Restoration it had passed to the FitzHerberts of Tissington, who added a wing in brick and Keuper Sandstone to designs by George Eaton of Etwall. The diplomat Lord St. Helen's was born here in 1754 and took his title from it. The artist Joseph Wright had it on a 21 year lease in 1772 and in 1800 it was sold to the marble manufacturer Richard Brown (1736-1816) who demolished it, advertising the materials for sale as from "the house in King Street, late Wright's". A new marble works was built in its place, today threatened by a new road scheme.

Haslebarrow Hall, Norton

Private collection, from a painting of the house of late 18th century date *(2001)*

William Selioke built a new house here in the 1570s, later taxed on 11 hearths, suggesting that it was of some pretension. Later it passed through the Freschevilles to the Morewoods, the Storeys and from them to John Wingfield, under whom it was a secondary house on the Norton House estate. He let it to the Jenkin family in 1729, but died in 1732, leaving a daughter and heiress through whom it came to the Newtons of Mickleover. They demolished it in 1810 when the Jenkin family died out and replaced it with a nearby farmhouse.

Eaton Dovedale Hall

M. Craven, woodcut from Tilley's Old Halls, Manors and Families of Derbyshire Vol. II (1893) *(2001)*

Although Joseph Tilley illustrated this house with this contemporary woodcut, it is almost certainly retrospective, as the house was reported as "ruinous" in 1789 and appears to have been reduced to little more than a heap of Keuper Sandstone rubble by 1811 after a lengthy period as a tenanted farm. It was built in 1576 for William Milward, from whose posterity it passed in the mid 18th century (when it ceased to be fully lived in) to the Clarkes of Ashgate and thence to the 1st Marquess of Ormonde, under whom it was demolished.

49

Swanwick Hall

M. Craven, from an engraving of late 18th century date   **(2001)**

In 1690, John Turner, a local coal owner, built a stylish new house of Coal Measure Sandstone, which was bequeathed to his son's business partner Anthony Tissington FRS in 1736. Not long after 1791 it was sold to the Woods, who had built a new villa nearby 20 years earlier (the present Hall) and when a tenancy lapsed in 1812, it was demolished as redundant.

Middleton Hall, Middleton-By-Youlgreave

Private collection, drawing datable to 1820   **(2001)**

In the 12th century, Robert Colle had a house here with a chapel, which passed to the Harthills and thence to the Cokaynes. A new house was built in Ashover Grit, in 1626, for Robert Bateman, and this was partly replaced by a rebuilding of c. 1790. It was gutted by fire around 1814 and demolished in July 1824 by Thomas Bateman, to be replaced by the present hall, on a new site.

Foston Hall*

Sir Howard Colvin, copied in 1848 from a drawing by Charles Sneyd Edgeworth dated 1816   (2001)

There was a series of seats at Foston, a 17th century one built for Sir Charles Agard being replaced around 1810 for John Broadhurst by a stylish Regency brick house of 7 by 5 bays and two storeys. The architect could well have been the Derby-born George Moneypenny, junior. In 1830 it was let to Colonel Charles Thorold Wood when it burned to the ground, not being replaced until 1863.

Langley Hall, Kirk Langley

D. F. Raybould, Esq,: 18th century sketch of the medieval house   (2001)

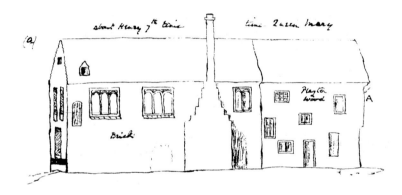

After the break-up of the original Langley estate with the failure of the male line of the Meynells, Sir Robert Twyford built a new house of Keuper Sandstone sometime after 1346, passing to the Poles in the 16th century. A century later the house appears to have been largely abandoned until 1669 when the Meynells bought it back. In 1758 an heiress carried it to Gilbert Chesshire who reduced it.

D. F. Raybould, Esq, a view of the house in the early 19th century   (2001)

The hall was first much reduced and partly remodelled shortly after 1758 in order to turn it into a farmhouse for Alderman Gilbert Chesshyre of Derby, and is seen here about the time Reverend Henry Peach inherited it in 1809 on the death of another absentee heir, Robert Cheney of Ashford. It was all swept away in 1833-34 when his son, Thomas, replaced it with the present hall.

Castlefields, Derby

M. Craven, detail from S & N Buck, East Prospect
of Derby *1728*   (2001)

Castlefields was built 1712-13 by Isaac Borrow (died 1745) Mayor of Derby in 1730 and 1742, not long after the death of his father, John. Typically Queen Anne, it was of brick with dressings of Ashover Grit or Rough Rock from Coxbench. The family, having altered the spelling of their name to Borough, removed to Chetwynd Park, Salop., in 1803, gradually disposing of their Derby estate for building. The house was let but lay empty for two years from 1836 before succumbing to the wrecking crew.

Derby Museum, view by china painter
George Robertson of c. 1800   (2001)

The gardens were geometrically laid out, but later re-designed – perhaps by William Emes – in a less formal style, seen here around 1800, looking south. From 1838 the site was built over, this avenue becoming Park Street, lined with terraces of artisans' cottages. The outbuildings remained until the 1890s, converted as a school.

Grangefield

Photograph in Introduction (Fig7, p.16)   (2001)

A fairly substantial timber framed seat was built at Grangefield (so named because it had once been a grange of the Abbey of Croxden, Staffordshire, by the gift of Robert de Beaufoy of Trusley) by Charles Hope after 1561. In about 1715 it passed by marriage to the Doxeys of Snelston, under whom it became a tenanted farm. It was eventually sold to the Strettons, but passed to the Trusley estate, the Strettons remaining as tenants, and was replaced between 1846 and 1848.

Chellaston Manor House

J. Mellor, reconstruction drawing from inventories, etc   (1984)

Chellaston Manor was a moderate sized timber-framed house probably built by the Ashby family in the later 15th century, altered and extended by the Whinyates family after 1622. About two centuries later, and stripped of its "considerable estate", it was split into cottages before being dismantled shortly before 1850, when the oak staircase was transferred to the *Red Lion* in the village, itself later demolished. The site was built over from 1957.

Ogston Hall (II)

Derbyshire Record Office by kind permission of Gladwin Turbutt, Pickford's entrance front elevation of 1768

(2001)

The Turbutt family came to Ogston in 1717 by marriage with the heiress of Revel, who had rebuilt their 16th century house in 1659. In 1768, Joseph Pickford of Derby built a new villa-style house for William Turbutt, to replace much of the old house, in Coal Measure Sandstone, like its predecessor. In 1850-52, Gladwin Turbutt built a new house to the designs of Thomas Chambers Hine of Nottingham, who retained most of the shell of Pickford's house, but gutted the interior entirely and clad the exterior with a bravura cloak of Neo-Jacobean detail, utterly transforming it.

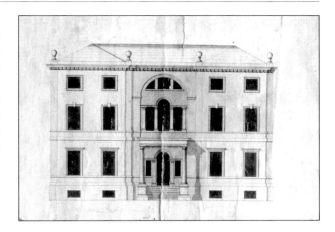

Exeter House, Derby

M. Craven, photograph of autumn, 1853 by Richard Keene   *No entry*

The largest house in Derby was originally a more modest early 17th century affair, radically enlarged after the Restoration in brick by John Bagnold, MP. His son-in-law Thomas Chambers re-fronted in around 1712 and his son-in-law, 8th Earl of Exeter was host *in absentia* to Bonnie Prince Charlie 4-6th December 1745. It passed through several hands after 1758, and was sold for demolition in 1854 after some months of dereliction.

Stapenhill House

M. Craven, from S & N Buck, East Prospect of Burton *1732*   *(2001)*

Charles Blount built a "pretty good house on the banks of the Trent" here in the late 17th century, but it was sold to the Derby merchant Paul Ballidon around 1706. By 1827 it was the home of Thomas Allsopp of the brewing family who sold to the Clays, but it was demolished and replaced by Reverend John Clay before 1857, when the house (which may have incorporated parts of its predecessor, see chapter 6) was finished.

King's Newton Hall

M. Craven, postcard view of the ruins by Edward Martin of c. 1904   *(2001)*

Nicholas Hardye came by land here and built a house sometime after 1564. His grandson Henry Hardinge (as they later spelt their name) enlarged it in the early 17th century, only for Robert Hardinge to start again immediately after the Civil War, in Ashover Grit. His traditional gabled house, on which he paid tax on 11 hearths, was destroyed by fire in 1859 when let to Robert Green, and remained a burnt out shell for over 50 years.

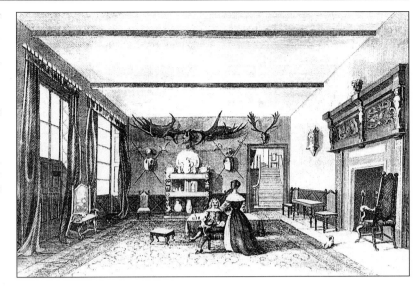

It is clear from this interior view of the hall that there must have been some 18th century alterations, hence the shutters and simple mahogany stick-balustered staircase. The house passed from the Hardinges to the Cokes of Melbourne in 1729, and it was let continuously thereafter, to the Mundys, Abneys and Jenneys. The house was entirely rebuilt in an Arts-and-Crafts interpretation of the original for George Edward Paget 1908-1910.

Spinkhill Hall, Eckington

In the mid-16th century, George, second son of John Pole of Wakebridge Hall acquired Spinkhill through his wife, Ellen, daughter and heiress of Richard Hazlehurst. He is said to have entirely rebuilt the house, which was taxed on 7 hearths in 1670. His descendant, John, died in 1724 when it came to the equally Catholic Morphys of Healey Hall, Yorkshire. His descendant, Pole Morphy of Kilkenny gave it to the Jesuits who founded the present Mount St. Mary's College there in 1842, much of the ancient seat being sacrificed to new buildings in 1859.

Burnaston Old Hall

Derby Local Studies Library, from a woodcut of earlier 19th century date   (1984)

A timber-framed house of probably 16th century origin, with a three gabled front, the central one being recessed, and later brick stacks. Anciently it was a seat of the Boningtons of Bearwardcote, and Ralph Bonington, a younger son, probably had it built. In 1630 it passed to the Brownes of Etwall but from 1732 it was let and was ultimately sold as a farmhouse, under the will of Isaac Hawkins Browne, to the Cottons of Etwall, the proceeds going towards the building of the Derbyshire General Infirmary. It was sold to the Smiths in the mid 19th century and demolished and replaced before 1892.

Rowtor Hall, Birchover

Derby Museum, view of 1859 photographed by Richard Keene   (2001)

Stephen Eyre of the Hassop family purchased an estate here in 1564, building the stone L-shaped house from nearby Ashover Grit not long afterwards. After the Restoration, his great grandson included it in a romantically contrived landscape, adding rock-cut seats, a small obelisk, lake and detached chapel. In 1717 it was sold to the Bradleys but later became united with the Stanton Hall estate, the old house being abandoned from the 1830s. It was pulled down as a ruin in 1870 and a vicarage was built in its place.

Thornbridge Hall

William Craven, vignette of 1871 from the sale catalogue   *(2001)*

Thornbridge was long part of the Little Longstone estate of the long-established Longsdon family. James Longsdon, who had built a classical house there in rustic Palladian, was in partnership in Manchester with Andrew Morewood, to whom he sold the house and some land in 1790, whereupon the latter added another range to it at right angles. His posterity eventually sold it to John Sleigh of Leek, who put it on the market in 1871. It was bought by another Mancunian businessman, Frederick Craven, who immediately demolished it and replaced it with a Neo-Jacobean house, since radically altered.

Crich Manor House

M. Craven, view of c. 1850 from S. T. Hall, Days in Derbyshire *(1863)*   *(2001)*

From the 14th century there must have been a capital mansion of the Belers family here, but by the beginning of the 17th century it had passed to the Clays, who built an L-shaped Jacobean house of local Ashover Grit. This appears to have undergone a thorough-going rebuild when the Flints inherited from the Brailsfords, the Clays' heirs, before 1712.

M. Craven, view of c.1850 from Hall, S.T. op.cit.   *(2001)*

A vignette of part of what must have been an impressive late 17th century plaster ceiling. The house later passed to the Saxtons, who seem to have demolished one wing entirely, and the grounds had been built over by as early as 1839. In 1875 it was almost entirely demolished, having been sold to the local Baptist congregation for a new chapel for £660, although fragments remain built into surrounding buildings.

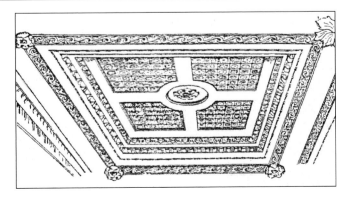

Twyford Old Hall

Derby Museum, from a drawing of c. 1871

(2001)

A manor house appears to have been built in timber here by the Crewkers, and this came via the Fyndernes to the Harpurs. A cadet of the latter, George Harpur, appears to have added a new range in a mixture of Keuper and Millstone Grit Sandstones in the early 17th century. Subsequent portions were added thereafter in timber and brick, probably to compensate for the loss, before 1670, of the medieval great hall, which George's son appears to have demolished or turned into a barn. From the 18th century it became a farmhouse, but in the 1870s suffered a major reduction, including the loss of all its timber framed portions, for adaptation as two labourers' cottages. What remains has since become a single residence again.

Coney Green Hall, North Wingfield*

C. Williams, from a photograph of 1883

(2001)

In the early 1760s, a mid-17th century farmhouse was transformed into a slightly gawky Palladian mansion in a small park by Francis Brailsford, who sold it in 1772 to Thomas Fanshawe and he within two years to the Wilsons. George Banks Wilson sold it to the Clay Cross Company in 1873, who installed their bailiff and tipped slag on the park. Undermined by subsidence, it was demolished to extend coal mining in April 1890.

The Grove, Darley Dale

James Darwin, view from a sale catalogue of 1876 (2001)

John Alsop of Lea Wood, an up-and-coming lead merchant, constructed a modest classical villa here about 1820. His homonymous grandson added matching wings on either side and a pediment to the original block, creating a handsome seat in 50 acres of parkland. It was later the home of Reverend. W. H. Bathurst and Robert Pringle before being sold to Manchester businessman William Roberts who, in 1884, pulled it all down and replaced it with a large Victorian house, later a hydro, now St. Elphin's School.

New Hall, Castleton

Mellors & Kirk, from a painting of c. 1800 *No entry*

Records of this house are hard to come by, but the illustration shows the surviving cross-wing of Carboniferous Limestone rubble of a late 15th century house with a late 18th century farmhouse attached, like Hazlebadge Hall in reverse. It seems to have been built by Thomas Savage, a scion of the house of Rocksavage, around 1480 and was decorated and improved c. 1560/70. It descended in his family until the Civil War when Royalism and poverty combined to force the sale of the estate to Rowland Morewood of Staden. From him it descended to the Halls, a Castleton family, who reduced and converted it, before attorney Joseph Hall sold it for the building of a Wesleyan Chapel in 1890 whereupon it was demolished.

Repton Park

Private collection, photograph by Richard Keene c. 1870 *(2001)*

Built as a castellated hunting lodge for Sir Henry Harpur Bt., of Calke in the 1620s, probably to a design by John Smythson. It was modernised by Samuel Brown of Derby in 1811, having already had its park breathtakingly landscaped, perhaps by Emes. It was then settled on a junior branch of the family, but was ordered to be torn down out of spite by Sir Vauncey Harpur-Crewe, Bt., after an altercation about butterfly hunting in the grounds in July 1893.

M. Craven, June 1990 *(2001)*

Brown's improvements included a service wing (hidden in trees), Gothic portico, re-fenestration, new hipped roof and some adjustment of the interior spaces. After the destruction of the house the park remains, wildly overgrown, as does the ruins of the castellated gatehouse range of 17th century date, part of which is seen here.

Littleover Old Hall

Miss F. Wright, from a watercolour of c. 1880 (2001)

A fairly substantial house was built here shortly after 1580 by Sir Richard Harpur and it passed in 1754 to Samuel Heathcote of Derby. They moved away in the 19th century, and the house was reduced drastically, and a brick farmhouse range added. The estate was sold in 1897 and Edward MacInnes demolished the old house and built a new one on the site.

Babington House, Derby

M. Craven, rear photograph of 23 July 1897 by J. Willatt of Derby *No entry*

A particularly handsome brick house with dressings of Keuper Sandstone built in 1626 for Henry Mellor of Idridgehay, later Derby's first Mayor. It was later the property of the Wilmots of Chaddesden (chapter 5), the Sitwells – then being called Sitwell Hall – and the Eyres before falling upon leaner times, and being demolished by Cllr Fletcher of the Public Benefit Boot & Shoe Co. in July 1897 for a grandiose retail scheme.

4

Houses destroyed 1900-1914

Brailsford Hall

M. Craven, from an earlier photograph by Richard Keene in Cox, W., The Pedigree of Cox *(1889)*   *(2001)*

William Cox, a Derby lead merchant, bought a modest estate here from 5th Earl Ferrers and re-built a "rather neglected" but substantial brick farmhouse, installing Robert Peach as tenant. Around 1810, his son remodelled it as a seat, probably to designs of the amateur architect Alderman Richard Leaper of Derby. It was sold to the Strutts of Belper in 1902 who demolished it and replaced it with a substantial new house, itself soon afterwards destroyed by fire and again rebuilt.

Hoon Hall

M. Craven, woodcut from J. Tilley, The Old Halls, Manors & Families of Derbyshire *(1893)*   *(2001)*

Hoon Hall was brick built in 1624 by one of the Palmers of Church Broughton, but was sold to the Staffords in the Civil War and in 1650 to Sir Robert Pye, 1st Bt. It passed to the Severnes in 1734 and in 1787 to the Watkins of Aynho Park, who adapted it as a farm house with vernacular fenestration and a coat of stucco. The estate was sold in the 1830s to the Locketts of Clonterbrook (Cheshire) and under them it was farmed by the Ormes and the Mellors. It was all sold in 1907 to Edmund Maynard from Chesterfield, who demolished it and built Hoon Ridge nearby, replacing it with a small modern farmhouse.

Romiley Hall, Clowne (II)

The late B F J Pardoe, from a painting by S. H. Grimm, c. 1792 *(2001)*

The de Boscos (or Woods, kin to the Sitwells) built a house here by 1455, of Coal Measure Sandstone, which passed to the Routhes under whom it seems to have been reduced to a modest farmhouse. Early in the 18th century it came to the Wrights and thence c. 1780 to Daniel Hill, who probably employed William Lindley of Doncaster to build a stylish Neo-Classical villa and Reverend Christopher Alderson to landscape the park. It all passed to Mrs Alfred Olivier of Derby and on her death in 1910 was sold to the Butler-Bowdons who destroyed the house.

M. Stanley, the surviving fragment of the Tudor house, 1983 *(2001)*

When the house was built, a part of the late medieval/early Tudor house was retained as a service wing, and this survived the destruction to become a byre, but it too became ruinous from the 1940s. Note the lighter dressing of Permian Magnesian Lime-stone on the doorcase in this house of coursed rubble Coal Measure Sandstone.

Norton House*

M. Craven, from a photograph possibly by Richard Keene c. 1870   *(2001)*

Built originally on a small estate by Leonard Gill in 1623, this house came via a number of heiresses to John Wingfield of Haslebarrow (cf. chapter 3) in 1712. In 1729 it passed to Robert Newton of Mickleover who modernised the east and south fronts in a manner recalling that of Wheston Hall (cf. chapter 8), but retained much interior panelling and several chimneypieces.

M. Craven, from Armitage, H., Chantry Land (1910) after a drawing of c. 1870   *(2001)*

A view of the un-rebuilt west front. The owners from 1789 were the Cunliffe Shawes and tenants included Thomas Beard Holy of Sheffield followed by Edward Montague Earle Welby (died 1926). He left on his retirement as a stipendiary magistrate in Sheffield not long before the Great War, whereupon it was sold for its materials and demolished.

5

Houses destroyed
1918-1929

Hasland House

M. Craven, from a postcard of 1914   *No entry*

A rather fine brick house built for Bernard Lucas (1708-1771) on his coming of age in 1729 by his father, ex-Chesterfield butcher, Thomas. On Bernard's younger grandson's death in 1818, the house was sold to Josiah Claughton (died 1838) a Chesterfield druggist, the last of whose four unmarried daughters, Catherine, died in the 1890s. In 1912 it was bought by Alderman George Albert Eastwood of Chesterfield and incorporated in a public park opened in July 1913. In 1914 a village hall, seen on the right was built alongside, but no real use was found for the house and it was demolished at the end of the Great War.

Aston Lodge, Aston-On-Trent*

M. Craven, from Briscoe, J. P., Nottinghamshire and Derbyshire at the Beginning of the Twentieth Century *1900*

(2001)

A house of the 1730s built for Joseph Greaves. His heirs, the Sneyds, sold it to James Sutton, the Shardlow canal entrepreneur, who added a full height bow to the garden front and a large extension on either side which did it few favours aesthetically. It was subsequently demolished after finding no tenant for a housing development in 1921. The fine Bakewell Gates, moved to West Park in Long Eaton in 1934, bear the later monogram RB (Reginald Boden, the last owner) on the overthrow, and may well have been transferred from Thomas Rivett's house in The Morledge, Derby in the 1900s.

Sutton Scarsdale (I)

M. Craven, from a postcard postmarked 1906

(2001)

One of the most important houses in the county, Sutton Scarsdale was built (incorporating the core of its predecessor) in 1724-7 for Nicholas Leake, 4th Earl of Scarsdale by Francis Smith of Warwick, using Top Hard Rock from the estate. It was sold to the Clarkes from whom it passed to the Marquess of Ormonde by whose heirs it was sold to the Arkwrights, who abandoned it after the Great War when a contractor gutted it in 1921. The shell was saved from demolition by Sir Osbert Sitwell in 1950.

The Sitwells gave the ruin of the house, then still hemmed in by coal mines, to the Nation in 1969, and it has since been consolidated and can be visited.

M. Stanley, a view through the north front, 1981 (2001)

Several of the rooms were carefully removed and shipped to the Philadelphia Museum in the USA in the 1920s. Fragments of stucco can still be seen within, as can parts of the house built just prior to 1595 by Sir Francis Leake.

Allen Hill, Matlock

C. Knowles, Mr. Slack and family enjoying the view, c. 1880   *(2001)*

A very modest sized 16th century manor house in Ashover Grit, which probably started out as a long house with, hall, to which was added a porch and cross-wing in 1653. Built for a junior branch of the Woolleys of Riber Hall, and passed to the Wolley-Dods (*sic*) of Edge Hall, Cheshire in 1827. They later let it – lastly to Mr. Slack, a Matlock butcher – but it fell into dereliction before succumbing to a new hydro in 1921.

Wirksworth Hall

R. S. Innes-Smith, the entrance front in 1910   *(2001)*

A house built by the Hurts in the 1720s was replaced by an ambitious villa by Joseph Pickford of Derby for Charles Hurt FRS in 1780. Only the Bakewell Gates survived from its predecessor, which are now at Henley Hall, Salop. Charles Hurt, banker, astronomer and bibliophile, was succeeded by his sons, their heirs the Hubberstys and the Price Woods, who retired to Henley Hall (taking the Bakewell Gates with them) in 1921. A speculator bought and demolished it the following year. A contemporary dower house survives.

Built for a cadet branch of the Foljambes of Walton before 1588 and altered by the Parliamentarian Colonel Gill after 1633, the house was sold to the Heywoods from whom it descended to the Cokes of Debdale Hall, Nottinghamshire, who, early in the 19th century, converted it into "small tenements occupied by labourers". This view shows the entrance front early in the 20th century when the house had been re-habilitated as the residence of the manager of the Staveley Company.

D. Coke-Steel, from a photograph by Richard Keene (2001)

The garden front in the 1870s when the house was occupied by Coke family kinsman Francis Sacheverell Wilmot. The house had been restored about 1831, but was left unoccupied after the death in 1918 of Henry Westlake, Staveley Co. manager. The Company demolished it in 1924, the outbuildings and walls following in 1931. There was fine "Sheffield School" plasterwork within.

M. Craven, photograph taken on acquisition by the Royal Society of Medicine 1924 (1984)

A surprisingly large villa built on land acquired from the Strutts in 1811 to designs by the Derby amateur architect, Alderman Richard Leaper (1759-1838). The client was a rich silk throwster, Thomas Bridgett, on whose death in 1841, his son Joseph sold it to Lord Belper, who installed three of his maiden aunts. It was set in a 70 acre park, which fell away sharply towards the Derwent from the irregular garden front, seen here.

Mrs. P. Lander, entrance in the 1870s, photographed by Richard Keene (1984)

Originally called Darley Grove, the name was changed in the 1840s to avoid confusion with the house of that name in Darley Dale (see chapter 3).

The house boasted Leaper's favourite cast iron sliding jalousies which, with the stair balusters, were cast nearby at Weatherhead, Glover & Co. The entrance front, seen here, was more compact than the east side. Lord Belper sold in 1880 to William Worthington who began to develop the southern portion of the park with housing.

South angle of the drawing room incorporating a later canted bay. The house passed through several hands until 1903 when it was purchased by lace manufacturer William Fletcher, on whose widow's death in 1922 it was sold to the Royal Society of Medicine for conversion to a medical facility. However, after lying empty for two years, it was demolished in 1924 and the site built over.

Farnah Hall, Duffield

The late Viscount Scarsdale, E. front c. 1880, from a photograph in a family album
compiled by Richard Keene (2001)

A plainish five bay three storey villa built in brick and Keuper Sandstone in 1736-8 for John Coape. It has been attributed by Professor Andor Gomme, who suspects it incorporated part of an existing house, to Francis Smith of Warwick. A large Regency extension of two storeys was added around 1820 for Hon. Nathaniel Curzon, whose father, Lord Scarsdale, had acquired the estate. The square bay was added in 1850.

The house was set in a landscaped park – conceivably laid out for the Coapes by William Emes, who was working at Kedleston from 1758 – with a lake, now filled in, but seen here in a 19th century view. The house became redundant after 1857 and had numerous tenants from then until 1916. The land, including Champeyne Park moat (see section I), remains in Curzon hands and part of the Kedleston estate.

After 1916 the house enjoyed only occasional use. No tenants could be found and it was abandoned in 1925. The Home Guard used it for Grenade practice during the War and it is now a complete ruin hidden in woodland, although the shell of the stable block remains to full height.

Chaddesden Hall

An estate at Chaddesden was acquired by the Wilmots in 1539 and a house of c.1626 was replaced in 1727-8 for Robert Wilmot, possibly to designs by Richard Jackson of Armitage, Staffordshire. It was in brick with dressings of Rough Rock and the central three bays were altered by Sir Robert Wilmot, 3rd Bt. after he succeeded in 1793.

Sir Robert's alterations included the creation of a remarkably ugly full height rear projection, seen here. On the death of the 6th baronet in action in 1918, the title and estate passed to a kinsman, the house was shut and all was sold for re-development in 1926. The house was then demolished although some of the park survives as a public open space.

Abbott's Hill, Derby

M. Craven, photograph by C. B. Sherwin of 1926 *No entry*

A tall brick house built c. 1720 in a park on an eminence overlooking the town by Dr. Simon Degge, FRS, FSA (1694-1729) in the plainer manner of Francis Smith of Warwick. It was sold in 1738 to the Foresters, kin to the Mundys of Markeaton (see section 7), and they sold it to an opulent maltster, Robert Foreman of Chellaston, then Mayor. In 1888 lace manufacturer Walter Boden acquired it, extensions by Alexander MacPherson being added, but his successor W. H. Richardson, a tanner, sold it for a large retail development in 1926 and it was demolished.

Wingerworth Hall

Having demolished the early Jacobean Villa. (see chapter 3) Sir Thomas Windsor Hunloke 3rd Bt. raised a fine new house of ashlared Coal Measure Sandstone (Deep Hard Rock) in "rustic Baroque" and attributable to Francis Smith of Warwick 1727-29, but leaving in place the service and chapel wings of the previous house. It survived until, after passing through three female lines, the family decided to abandon it, but by which time the view from its windows was dominated by the Clay Cross Colliery and a steelworks.

The north front, from the lake. The two lower projections either side of the central five bays are the surviving extensions of the former house. The ground floor central part was added by William Baker of Audlem in 1753-4. From the 1890s the house was let to Charles Allen and later to Col. Sir Charles Seeley, Bt., MP.

The interior was well supplied with bravura Baroque stucco, probably by Guiseppe Artari, as in this picture of the saloon, a 32 ft cube of some gandeur embellished with an eclectic Composite order. Philip Hunloke failed to find a tenant after the Great War and the house failed to sell in 1920. By 1927 it had been acquired by local contractor William Twigg who demolished it for the materials in 1928.

Derby Museum, photograph from a glass slide by Richard Keene of Derby, c. 1878.   *(2001)*

As with most houses by Francis Smith, the staircase was a resplendent example of the joiner's art, in this case that of Thomas Eborall. When the house was demolished one room went to St. Louis Museum, USA, where it was butchered to fit a smaller shape. The stairs and three other rooms were offered for sale by Robersons of Knightsbridge, but it is not known what became of them.

6
ℋouses destroyed
1930-1939

Cliffe House, Newton Solney

Private collection, photograph of 1928   No entry

A substantial Neo-Jacobean mansion built in 1859-60 on a 12 acre plot by the Trent for Samuel Ratcliffe of a Burton-on-Trent brewing dynasty. The architect was Robert Grace of Burton-on-Trent. Ratcliffe's son-in-law married an aunt of the late Sir John Betjeman. Samuel's younger son inherited but in 1877 bought Newton Park, leaving the house to his unmarried sisters.

Staircase hall with cantilevered Hoptonwood stone staircase and quirky locally-cast iron balustrade. After the last of Ratcliffe's sisters had died, in 1908, the house was let to Percy Kent Le May, but after he left in 1928 no tenant could be found. It failed to sell at auction in March 1929 and was demolished as redundant a year later.

The drawing room, which boasted an impressive white Cararra marble chimneypiece and an elaborate plaster cornice. Mr Le May's furniture was hardly of the epic scale required for such an ambitious house!

Stable block and coach house, although the latter had become a motor house by the 1920s. Like the house itself, it was all built of brick with dressings of Keuper Sandstone. The site is still vacant, although the buildings depicted here largely survived and are now residences.

Netherseal Hall

M. Craven, from a print of a drawing by a member of the Gresley family dated April 24th 1855. (2001)

Gilbert Morewood built a tall house with a parapet, reminiscent of Tupton Hall in the 1620s. It was repeatedly modified by his heirs, the Gresleys. By 1855 it had been Georgianised very thoroughly with sash windows throughout and a plain brick service wing to the left.

J. Darwin, photograph of c. 1890 (2001)

In the third quarter of the 19th century, Rev. Nigel Gresley (father of locomotive engineer Sir Herbert Nigel Gresley) greatly enlarged it with a new wing at right angles and a row of inconsequential shaped gables replacing the parapet. A further rebuilding by Sir Reginald Blomfield was done in 1908-11, but by 1914 it was let. The Gresleys, later in decline, offered it for sale in 1927, and E. J. Manners bought it, but moved into the Old Hall in 1933 and demolished it, selling the site for building.

Stapenhill House

M. Craven, from a photograph of the 1890s   *(2001)*

The replacement of the house noticed in chapter 3 lasted less than 80 years, being "new" in 1857, when it was occupied by its builder Reverend John Clay. He had commissioned H. I. Stevens of Derby to build the new church nearby in 1837-8, so this house may also be by him. It was of brick with dressings of Keuper Sandstone, and may have incorporated part of the previous house. For almost forty years to 1930 it was home to the Goodgers, local attorneys, but it was sold in 1930 to Burton Corporation who demolished it in 1933 and turned the site into a public park.

Darley House, Darley Abbey

Derby Museum, 1931 photograph   *(2001)*

Darley House (at first called Darley Fields) was the original home of the Evanses, proprietors of the nearby Boar's Head cotton mill, and was built about 1790, quite possibly to a design by William Strutt FRS, a close kinsman. Coleridge stayed there, but from 1835, when the family acquired Darley Hall (see chapter 9) it was given over to aunts.

The dining room in about 1920. After the last of the Evans aunts died, the house was let to Colonel Charles Cavendish, but after 1918 it was let as a school. This folded in the recession, and all was sold to Derby Corporation in 1931, who demolished it in 1934 and later sold the 23 acre park for re-development.

Drakelow Hall*

M. Craven, steel engraving intended for Vol. III of Stephen Glover's History and Gazetteer of Derbyshire
(never published) from a painting by Henry Moore of c. 1830   *(2001)*

The Gresleys had had a seat here from very early on, but this house originated in one built in the 16th century with a long façade – closely akin to that at Longford – probably shortly after 1543. It was rebuilt in 1723 and by John Westmacott in 1806, who tried to return it to some Romantic semblance of its original appearance, as in this engraving. It was brick with Keuper Sandstone dressings.

M. Craven, a postcard view using a Richard Keene photograph of the 1860s   *(2001)*

A further remodelling took place in 1840 – to no good effect – leaving the house as seen in this view. However, it was further altered in the 1870s and again in 1901-4 by Sir Reginald Blomfield, who remodelled the interior and the Tudor entrance portico. Financial considerations forced its sale in 1931 and in 1934 Sir Clifford Gothard pulled it down, although Blomfield's portico went on to grace Syston Hall, Lincs.

Trompe Oeil dining room alcove by Paul Sandby, 1793, now in the V & A. Most of the other interiors were replaced in 1901 under Blomfield by Gregory & Co., George Jackson & Sons and W. Aumonier & Son. The site is now occupied by a very large power station.

Derby Museum, T. 501/J. Darwin: c. 1925 (2001)

The saloon, showing the interior approximately as it was following the 1840 re-modelling. Some of the contents were of exceptional quality and interest, and their dispersal at the 1931 sale was in itself a disaster.

The drawing room, which was unusual in a house of this size in being lit by only one window. This interior is Edwardian overlaid on an interior probably from the 1806 period.

The music room – an elongated octagon – one of the interiors surviving from the early 18th century and panelled in fashionable mahogany rather than oak.

Errwood Hall

An Italianate house set in an impossibly romantic setting above the Goyt Valley, designed by the Scots architect Alexander Roos and begun in 1841. The pleasure grounds were a show-place for the then newly-imported rhododendron and, running wild, they still dominate the landscape.

Errwood was commissioned by Lancastrian Catholic industrialist Samuel Grimshawe, and took until 1851 to complete. It was constructed of rock-faced ashlar in Millstone Grit (probably Rough Rock). Alexander Beresford Hope PRIBA designed a chapel, this view being his sketch to show its appearance, for it was never built, due to Grimshawe's death in 1851.

S. D. Grimshawe, who inherited the house in 1851, abandoned the chapel and built a family mausoleum instead, adapting a room in the house as the chapel. His heirs remained there until 1930 when the estate was sold to Stockport Corporation who let the house to the YHA until 1934 when it was abandoned and largely dismantled.

Risley Lodge

M. Craven, from a postcard by J. A. Martin, Stapleford. c.1904   No entry

A three bay Regency villa built in brick and Brookhouse's Roman Cement before 1827, quite possibly to the designs of Joseph Cooper of Derby, an attribution strengthened by the use of Weatherhead, Glover & Co.'s cast iron sliding jalousies.

It was let to lace manufacturer Benjamin Towle by 1827, but was a residence of the Pares of Hopwell Hall until 1894 (see chapter 8). It was then sold to Terah Hooley JP, a tenant since 1883, but later seems to have been mortgaged by his son, the failed financier, E. T. Hooley, forcing its sale in 1927. It was bought by Benjamin Bates, and burnt down during demolition c. 1934/5 and was replaced on the same site.

Alvaston Hall

Derby Museum, painting of c. 1920   (2001)

Alvaston Hall was built in the earlier 17th century by the Allestreys, whose heirs lost it by legal sleight-of-hand to the Boroughs of Castlefields in the 1740s. It was much rebuilt by Joseph Wheeldon in the 1820s. After many years as the seat of the Smiths, the coach builders, it was sold for re-development and demolished in March 1935.

Rose Hill, Chesterfield

Chesterfield Local Studies Library, view of 1936   *No entry*

The entrance front of this house was much like that of nearby West House (also gone) and quite possibly by the same builder. It is said it was built for the Thornhills, but it was rebuilt for Robert Lowndes before 1779, when the garden front was given an exceptionally well-proportioned five bay two and a half storey brick façade in the plain later style of Joseph Pickford, although work of this quality could just as easily have been by John Carr of York, who designed the Guildhall here in 1787. The earlier date might favour Pickford who worked nearby at Ogston (qv) in 1768. From 1860 it was the house of John Brown of Cutthorpe Hall, agent to the Wingerworth estate, but both were in the hands of Frederick Butcher by 1891 (probably his heir) and his family still owned it when it was demolished in 1936 to make way for Chesterfield's new Town Hall.

Bridge Hill House, Belper

J. Darwin, from a postcard of c. 1904   *No entry*

1938 was a bad year for country houses. It saw the demolition of this quite substantial Regency mansion built in 1793-4 for George Benson Strutt and designed by him and his brother, William, to incorporate a variety of the latest "domestic economy" devices. It was extended about a decade later. It remained with G. B. Strutt's descendants until the death of the widow of George Herbert Strutt in 1931, when the contents were sold in December. No tenants could be found for it (the view from it was exclusively of former Strutt family mills) and it went in 1938.

Doveridge was a magnificent late Palladian seat built from 1770 for Sir Henry Cavendish, 1st Bt., PC (I) to designs by Edward Stephens. Two pavilions attached by single storey wings were then added by the contractor, Joseph Pickford of Derby. In the late 19th century Cavendish's descendant, 4th Lord Waterpark let it, later selling to 1st Lord Hindlip. It was effectively redundant later, and was sold to a "developer" in 1935 for £4,000 who demolished it in 1938.

Not only was the interior magnificent, but the entrance front – largely in brick rather than the Keuper Sandstone of the river front – was mainly designed by Pickford, who took over when Stephens died in 1774. Here the Meynell Hunt is seen foregathering in 1905. The site is now largely built over.

Culland Hall

M. Craven, photograph by Richard Keene of c. 1888 from Cox, W. Pedigree of Cox of Derbyshire, 1889   *(2001)*

The late Colonel Sir Edward Thompson (1907-1994) bought the Culland estate in 1938 from the Walkers, under whom the much rebuilt brick 17th century seat of the Drapers had been tenanted as a farm. From them it had descended to the Portes of Ilam who sold it to William Cox of Brailsford Hall (qv chapter 4) in 1794. It was entirely replaced by Sir Edward with a rather splendid new neo-classical house by George Eaton of Derby incorporating the pedimented entrance of the old house.

Heanor Hall

M. Craven, from a postcard of c. 1910   *(2001)*

A fine, later 17th century brick house with the entrance in its long side and embellished with shaped gables on the returns, built by the Ropers around 1690. It was re-fenestrated and somewhat enlarged in the later 18th century by John Sutton, who bought it from the Fletchers. It passed to the Rays in 1803, was later tenanted and given as the focus of the new Heanor Technical School in 1906. It was replaced by more up-to-date structures in 1938.

Osmaston Hall, Osmaston-By-Derby

M. Craven, photograph by Richard Keene of c. 1859 later adapted as a postcard (2001)

1938 saw the demolition of this fine seat of the Wilmots, Bts., after a long decline, exacerbated by the encroachment of industrial Derby. It was built of brick with dressings of Keuper Sandstone to designs of Sir William Wilson in 1696 (incorporating part of its predecessor, see chapter 1) for Robert Wilmot MP. Sir Robert Wilmot, 1st Bt. added Palladian pavilions on the entrance front, Bakewell Gates (his last) and had William Emes lay out the parkland with its lake.

Derby Museum, by permission of Miss Kimpton, Richard Keene photograph (2001)

The drawing room, with a view into the dining room beyond, c. 1875. The main apartments were richly furnished with panelling and bolection surrounds to the doorcases and chimneypieces. The house was let in 1814 to Alderman Samuel Fox of Derby, whose descendants lived there until 1887.

When he took over, Alderman Fox persuaded his colleague, the prolific amateur architect, Alderman Richard Leaper (1759-1838) to design lodges. This view is of the one of c. 1825 on Osmaston Road: *cottage ornée* with a dash of Gothick. It outlasted the house, going to make way for Ascot Drive in 1949.

Demolition proceeding, July, 1938. The house and grounds hosted the Royal Show in 1871, 1906, 1921 and 1933, but had been sold to the Midland Railway as offices and storage in 1888. It was re-sold, as surplus to requirements, by the LMSR to Derby Borough Council in 1938 and demolished by Messrs Ford & Weston, to be replaced (after the War) by an industrial estate.

Tupton Hall*

M. Craven, from an early 19th century steel engraving. *(2001)*

This famous engraving of Tupton Hall is a real mystery. It shows a six-bay, three storey tower house of the right approximate date, with two four storey towers at each end and a continuous balustrade. Yet the house was of five by three bays, of five storeys at the ends and three string courses, not one. Either it was done from memory, or is actually of another of these intriguing Midlands high houses altogether. One inclines, now, to the latter view. Either way (and wherever it was) it is a lost Derbyshire House!

M. Craven, from a postcard of c. 1920 with the children of the tenant on the lawn *(2001)*

The house was built in Millstone Grit Sandstone, perhaps to a design by Robert or John Smythson, in 1611 for Thomas Gladwin, a Yorkshire gentleman who had his name and that of his wife Helen placed amidst the top balustrade. Around 1750 the house was thoroughly Georgianised, sashes replaced the tall windows on the first and ground floors and the east front was reduced from five to three floors. It passed from the Gladwins to the Allwoods and the Lords before sale to the Packman family in the 19th century.

NMR, dining room ceiling, c. 1931 *(2001)*

The alterations by Lemuel Gladwin included some fairly lavish Palladian chimneypieces and stucco, as here in the dining room centered on the arms of the Gladwins. The house was sold to the County Council in 1929 and opened as the Clay Cross Secondary School in 1936, but the old house was utterly destroyed by fire in July 1938, the shell being cleared the following year as unsafe.

St. Mary's Gate House, Derby

M. Craven, photograph by Richard Keene of Derby c. 1885 *No entry*

A magnificent quasi-Palladian mansion built by William Osborne in 1730-1 quite possibly to designs by James Gibbs, and embellished with a riot of fine wrought ironwork by Robert Bakewell, most of which has, mercifully, survived. It descended to Sir Hugh Bateman, Bt., of Hartington, who sold it to Thomas Evans of Darley House (see above) His grandson sold it for conversion as a Baptist chapel in 1842.

It became surplus to requirements in 1938 when it was sold to Sir George Kenning for demolition as a car-lot. The plain East wing partly survives.

West Hallam Hall

M. Burrows, from a photograph of c. 1895 (2001)

West Hallam Hall was originally a fairly large late medieval seat demolished by the Hunlokes in the 1770s. The Newdigates acquired the estate in 1822 but left it until 1876 to build a new house to the rather pedestrian design of John Parkin of Derby, essentially intended for the agent. It later had numerous tenants before being sold to Henry FitzHerbert Wright and in 1913 to Alderman Sir Albert Ball of Nottingham father of RFC hero, Albert Ball, V.C. It was demolished in 1938-9 for a housing estate.

The Eyres acquired the estate at Newbold in 1570, building a long-vanished seat, of which only the chapel, recently restored, survives. By the later 18th century, they had begun to break up their holdings there and 200 acres were sold to the Tomlinson family from whom it passed to Jonathan Bromehead of Eckington, whose son Alexander Crawford Bromehead built this modest stone house c.1780.

Four generations of Bromeheads lived at the house – which was much extended c. 1820 – the last of whom was Colonel N. J. E. Orange-Bromehead. His drawing room furnishings are shown here in 1905. When he left in 1911, the house was let, but by the early 1930s there were no more takers and it was demolished for re-development in 1938.

Windle Hill, Thurvaston*

Mrs. H. Walker, from a postcard of c. 1910 (2001)

A fairly ambitious but old-fashioned timber framed seat was built here in the 1660s by Robert Rowe on the site of an early Tudor house of the Mynors family, part of which was suffered to remain. The Newalls inherited it and in the 18th century extended it in brick. Under their heirs, the Portes of Ilam, it became a tenanted farm, reduced by demolition of the oldest part in the 19th century. It became redundant and derelict by the 1930s and was pulled down in 1939.

Ravenstone House

Private collection, from a 19th century watercolour No entry

An exceptionally well-proportioned but modest sized brick house with two full height canted bays set just in Derbyshire (but from 1887 in Leicestershire) and built in 1788 by Robert Creswell (died 1825), a member of an old local family grown rich from mineral extraction. The family retained the estate (part of which was rented from the Fosbrookes of Ravenstone Hall) until after the Great War when Richard Creswell succeeded his father and it was sold to Arthur Laxton-Hames. It was demolished in the later 1930s and the site later built over.

7

Losses in the 1940s

Longford Hall

M. Craven, The north and east ranges, later destroyed, postcard of c. 1906   (2001)

A massive brick house with Keuper Sandstone dressings of early Tudor date and architecturally related to Drakelowe (see chapter 6). It was built for the Longfords, and passed to the Cokes who held it (and had Pickford Georgianise it in 1762) until 1920 when Sir Charles Markham bought it. In 1942, the brewer H. Arthur Manners was there, but an entire range was destroyed in a serious fire. The shell was later removed apart from a small part of the NE angle. The remainder of the house was ultimately re-habilitated by the Barnes family.

Derwent Hall

M. Craven, South front as rebuilt, from a postcard franked 1907   *(2001)*

A rather modest and old fashioned manor house was built in the 1670s by Henry Balguy in coarsely ashlared Kinderscout Grit and re-modelled by his son in 1692. After two subsequent ownerships, it was sold in 1876 to the Duke of Norfolk, for whose younger son, later 1st Viscount FitzAlan of Derwent, it was vastly extended and modernized.

J. Darwin, from a perspective by Hanson in The Builder *27/8/1881*   *(2001)*

The architect for the improvements was Joseph Aloysius Hanson, who added a second E – W pile, a stable block and service wing to the north and two wings to the east, at the extremity of the southernmost of which he built a (Catholic) chapel of some grandeur. All bar the chapel were in matching style. It was let to the YHA from 1932-1938.

The new interiors were richly panelled with wainscot from other demolished houses, like old Norton Hall (see chapter 2) and a new, richly carved staircase was put in. It was finally doomed by plans to build Ladybower reservoir, and vacated in 1943, being largely dismantled by Charles Boot before disappearing under the waves in 1945. The panelling in this view of the new drawing room was eventually re-set in the Mayor's parlour, Derby Council House, opened in 1948.

Trusley Manor

P. Channon, photograph by Charles Barrow Keene of the house in snow, 1913 (2001)

The Cokes had held Trusley from the 14th century, but it passed out of the family between 1718 and 1818, by which time the original manor house had been reduced to a modest farmhouse. No new house was required until 1902 when Major General J. T. Coke built a large new house in Jacobean style of brick and Keuper Sandstone dressings to designs by F. Bowles of London and George Eaton, PRIBA of Derby.

The male line of this branch of the family was tragically wiped out in the Second World War, and the heirs, Mrs & Mrs Ronald Coke-Steel, were forced to demolish four fifths of the house in 1946. Only the range to the right in this view of 1912 survived as a dower house, now apartments. The family now reside in the Old Hall.

Shipley Hall

M. Craven, new west front, photographed by Cornelia, Countess of Craven, 8/4/1909 (2001)

One Shipley Hall took over where another one ended (see chapter 2). When the earlier seat was demolished in 1749, Edward Mundy's new house was "rising fast". Unfortunately, we have little idea of its appearance for, in 1778-9 it was rebuilt out of all recognition in neo-classical style to designs by William Lindley of Doncaster, before being enlarged in matching style by Sir Walter Tapper for Alfred Edward Miller-Mundy from 1895, as here.

M. Craven, photograph of 1909 by Cornelia,
Countess of Craven (2001)

The Italian Pergola created by Tapper and John Cragoe Tallack at the turn of the century. The latter succeeded William Elphinstone as head gardener in 1899 in the task of beautifying the gardens and grounds. The estate was at this time 2,789 acres, including the highly productive Shipley Colliery.

M. Craven, photograph of 1909 by Cornelia,
Countess of Craven (2001)

William Elphinstone's Fountain Walk, in 1908, with Lady Craven's mutt Zizi approaching. The Cararra marble fountain supported a lead figure by Derwent Wood, RA. In 1922, Godfrey Miller-Mundy, who succeeded in 1920, decided to sell the estate to the Shipley Colliery Company, to help defray death duties and move south, away from the industrial grime and pollution rapidly encroaching.

M. Craven, 1998 (2001)

In 1860-61 W. E. Nesfield was called in to build the turreted model farm and its dairy. The latter was Minton tiled and embellished with the *Four Seasons* in stained glass by H. J. Westlake, which survives in Shipley Country Park.

Nesfield also built the nearby water tower, listed II* and now a private house. The Colliery Company were unwise enough to extract coal from under the hall, and the resulting signs of subsidence deterred some potential purchasers. In 1948 it was unceremoniously demolished by the newly nationalised NCB, but what remained was purchased by the County Council as a country park in the 1970s. They later sold the model farm on.

Old Mayor's Parlour, Derby

M. Craven, postcard from an earlier photograph by Richard Keene, 1870s   *No entry*

When it was unceremoniously demolished by the Borough Council in 1948, this magnificent timber framed house, crammed at right angles to Tenant Street on a double burgage plot, was the largest urban timber-framed house of its period in Britain. It was constructed in or around 1483, although for whom is not now known.

By 1670 it was divided in two, one half being the residence of pioneer gynaecologist Dr Percival Willoughby. In the earlier 18th century, a Georgian street front was added, and by the 19th century the Gadsby family had let it to the Council as offices. Despite many pleas it went, the site being for many years a bus park, but is now part of the Sir Peter Hilton Memorial Garden.

Leek-born John Allcard, a rich stockbroker, built a house in Ashover Grit ashlar in 1845 on an estate purchased from the Duke of Rutland. It was designed by Sir Joseph Paxton and decorated by A. W. N. Pugin, and was the epitome of romantic early Victorian taste. There was Minton tiling, and stained glass by John Hardman (who also provided ironwork) with one other by Ford Maddox Brown.

RCHM (E), East front before the alterations of 1888, photograph by Keene   *(2001)*

Considerable additions were made by E. W. Pugin and T. D. Barry and further interior decoration by J. G. Crace from 1854, the work being taken over on Allcard's death by his son, W. H. Allcard, a notable locomotive engineer. From 1866 it was owned by Smith Taylor-Whitehead, who added a spectacular tower on the east side, designed by J. B. Mitchell-Withers, in 1888.

E. W. Pugin's orangery of 1854-5. The house failed to find a use after the death of Alexander Campbell-Blair in the 1930s, and was mis-treated during the war. A substantial portion was demolished in 1949, and the service accommodation in 1972 when an unsightly block of flats was put up on the site and Paxton's grounds covered with small boxy houses. What remains is now divided into residences.

Detail of the staircase and a stucco ceiling boss. Before its recent re-habilitation what remained of the house was derelict for a time and subject to an application to demolish, mercifully refused.

Sawley Manor

Derby Museum, after a watercolour of 1938　　　　　　　　　　　　*No entry*

Few will have taken much notice in the later 1940s when the old brick gabled house next to the *Nag's Head* at Sawley was demolished. It had long been split as separate cottages. Indeed what remained, right on the street front, was but a fragment of a larger house of the Stanhopes, Earls of Chesterfield, in existence by 1611. They lost it to John Pymme in 1650, but regained it, later selling to Sir William Leche of Shipley who paid tax on 10 hearths. It passed in 1732 to the Holdens of Aston; and had already been tenanted for some time then. Later, reduced and rebuilt, it belonged to the Madans but thereafter its history is obscure.

Stretton Hall, Stretton-en-le-Field*

M. Craven, engraving from Nicols' Leicestershire 1804　　　　　　　　*(2001)*

The Strettons were an ancient family, recorded here in 1086. Indeed, Edric de Stretton is said to have been notable for having been strangled and de–fenestrated into the Thames on the orders of King Canute in 1017! By the mid 16th century the estate had been acquired by John Browne of Horton Kirby, Kent, whose posterity a century later appear to have built a substantial brick gabled seat with Keuper Sandstone dressings. It passed in 1752 to the Caves, later Cave-

Browne-Cave, who had attained a baronetcy in the Civil War. The awkward looking full height bow seems to have been added in the 1790s.

L. F. Cave-Browne-Cave, garden front as rebuilt, photographed before 1861

The house, set in a 60 acre park, was enlarged by the addition of gabled extensions at either end and embellished with carved barge-boards in 1845, but was all sold up in 1912. It was demolished in June 1949 after the death of its last owner, Christopher Spalding, JP, and was later replaced by the present unappealing residence.

8

Losses in the 1950s

Field House, Spondon

M. Craven, photograph by Richard Keene of c.1870   *(2001)*

This important house was built for B.T. Balguy, shortly after his appointment as Town Clerk of Derby in 1818 and echoes the West front of Samuel Wyatt's Egginton Hall (see below). It stood at the site of a previous house owned by the Osbournes. There was a 13 acre park, the entrance to which was embellished from 1873 with the classical gate piers from St Helen's House. They were acquired by Frederick Arkwright who lived here from 1850 and who was governor of Derby School, then using the St Helen's House. Latterly owned by the Devas family, it was pulled down in the early 1950s.

Appleby Hall

M. Craven, postcard of c. 1905 (2001)

Thomas Gardner of Uttoxeter built this fine ashlar, 5 by 3 bay, two and a half storey house for George Moore in 1786 from the local Coal Measure Sandstone. T.C. Hine of Nottingham extended and renovated the house in the mid 19th century, but the Moores sold in 1920 and it was reduced in 1927. Ruinous by the late 1930s the whole house was removed in 1952 following problems with mining subsidence. Gardner's delightful rectory and its stable block remain, as does the 15th century gatehouse and bridge of the moated medieval timber-framed house of the Applebys, the Moores' predecessors, situated nearby.

Wheston Hall (II)

M. Craven, Richard Keene photograph of 1873 (2001)

This magnificent photograph by Richard Keene shows the house in 1873 in all its splendour. It was a late 16th century house, built by the Alleynes and taxed on 8 hearths in 1670. The recessional facade was Georgianized by an unknown architect for Thomas Freeman in about 1727. This view of the main entrance front obscures the earlier fabric, much of which survived at the rear. Freeman also laid out parkland and an avenue.

The house became part of the Duke of Norfolk's estate and later that of the Devonshires, under whom it became a farmhouse. Years of neglect took their toll when a severe gale caused the collapse of the west end of the north front in 1952.

This view of the south front shows clearly the earlier fabric on the right with the 1727 new build to the left. The lighter Carboniferous Limestone is brought to course with the darker Millstone Grit Sandstone used for the dressings. The roof is stone slate and, as with the walling, is all from the adjacent outcrop.

After the west end collapsed in 1952 the house remained as a semi-ruin until 1960. The east end was then demolished except for the NE angle, which was reduced to one storey. The top storey right across the house also disappeared. The east stair tower went leaving the western one to access the first storey. The introduction of 4 pane sashes on the main façade completed the transformation from an elegant 18th century large house to something reminiscent of an odd-looking Edwardian house.

Snelston Hall (II)

Derby Museum: drawing of 1843

(2001)

Lewis Cottingham's fourth design for John Harrison took 10 years to build, starting in 1827, and echoed Alton Towers just across the River Dove in Staffordshire. Buttresses ran up to end in a profusion of crocketed pinnacles. Above all, a two storey gabled, four centred entrance arch, with an oriel window was added to the Gothic fantasy. Nothing quite like it had been built before or since in the county.

Cottingham's first Gothic design for Harrison followed two previously rejected classical designs, one neo-Greek. This was a much more modest seven bay two storey house in a mild form of gothic, also drawn in 1827.

Cottingham's second Gothic design was even more extravagant, more church-like than his first design, but obviously still not exuberant enough for Harrison.

The house as finished can be seen between the trees. The interior was expensively impressive with knopped pendants on the great hall ceiling and an intricate oak staircase. Adam Bede of Norbury, whose name inspired the local George Eliot's central character, did much of the carving. The house passed from the Harrisons to the Stantons in 1906 and was demolished in 1953.

Willesley Hall

Basically a late 17th century Restoration house for James Abney, refaced in Keuper Sandstone by 1820 for his descendant, Sir Charles Abney-Hastings, 1st Bt., natural son of the 10th Earl of Huntingdon, it was radically altered in 1845 and sold by the Earl of Loudoun, the Hastings' heir in 1919, becoming an hotel in 1925. When the hotel closed in 1936 it became derelict, and was demolished in 1953.

The 1892 drawing shows the house as finally rebuilt after 1845, possibly by Edward Blore for Sir Charles Abney-Hastings 2nd Bt.

The park was landscaped in the late 18th century with linear walks and a 24 acre lake, drowning the village of Willesley. It was sold to the local golf club in 1921 who retain most of the land.

Eggington Hall

M. Craven, postcard of c.1916 (2001)

Built in 1782-3 by Samuel Wyatt for the Everys who had held it from 1622 when it passed by marriage from the Leighs. The "good house" of the Leighs was taxed on 22 hearths in 1670, but was burnt in 1736. Repaired by Benjamin Wyatt in 1756 and replaced completely by Samuel, who gave it a 9 bay entrance front seen here when it was a 1914-18 war military hospital.

NMR, 1954 (2001)

Samuel Wyatt had emphasised the length of the façade by paired bows at both east and west ends, those on the west end (seen here) flanking a subsidiary entrance.

The c.1700 park was laid out by Lawrence Squibb of Derby and was fully landscaped by William Emes with a new lake created from the River Dove and a cascade crossed by a Chinoiserie footbridge. This was replaced by one from the Coalbrookdale Company dated 1812 and today the 8th oldest cast iron bridge in Britain, now listed Grade II*.

Private collection, c. 1795 from a painting possibly by Henry Moore of Derby (2001)

William Emes completed the landscaping as seen in this oil painting of c.1795. He often worked with the Wyatts after the death of Joseph Pickford in 1782, with whom he had worked closely in the previous two decades. Sir John Every, Bt., pulled the house down in 1955 and sold the site. In 1994 Kevin Ellis, a Derby property developer, acquired the site and 17 acres of former park and in 1997 completed a new house there in Regency style with Adam Bench, for Derek Latham and Associates, as the architect.

Etwall Hall (II)

James Darwin, postcard of c. 1904   (2001)

Demolished in 1955 to make way for yet another school, this time the former Sir John Port Grammar School. The Portes (sic) were granted the estate after the Dissolution, but it was later held by the Gerards and Mosleys before Sir Samuel Sleigh rebuilt it in stone from Tutbury Castle in about 1643. Thereafter it sported 3 storey towers at the angles of the garden front.

Derbyshire Life and Countryside, 1955   (2001)

Taxed on 13 hearths in 1670, the house passed to the Chethams who had Francis Smith of Warwick rebuild it between 1713 and 1726 in ashlar Keuper Sandstone. This view of the house under demolition shows part of the Robert Bakewell wrought iron screen, the gates to which survived and can now be seen in front of Sir John Porte's almshouses by the church.

Old Ford House, Stretton-in-Shirland

G. Turbutt, postcard of c.1908   *(2001)*

This pretty two storey early 17th century house was Ford Old House, long the home of the Curteis family, who became Quakers and departed for New Jersey, America in 1680. The estate was sold to George Holland, whose maltster son John added a slightly taller range at right angles, originally as a malthouse. It later became the secondary house on the estate, but was unnecessarily demolished together with Ford House itself in 1957 to provide space for "reservoir houses" for Ogston reservoir.

Ford House, Stretton-in-Shirland

G. Turbutt, postcard of c.1908   *(2001)*

A pigeon house and a wall of the 18th century kitchen garden are all that remains of this severe 3-paired bay by 4, two and a half storey Coal Measure sandstone house built for maltster Thomas Holland. An undated receipt for £336 is dated by Gladwyn Turbutt to around 1723/4, although the architecture might suggest a decade later. The awkward pairing of the entrance and hall light under a rather formless floating pediment might suggest a local builder's attempt to be up-to-date.

In 1776 Thomas Holland was succeeded by his cultivated son John, a friend and pupil of Joseph Wright ARA and Reverend Thomas Gisbourne, through whom he made the acquaintance of Revd. William Mason and his friend the poet Thomas Gray. Mason was an intimate of Reverend Christopher Alderson, rector of Eckington, who laid out the gardens at Frogmore for Queen Charlotte, and the possibility exists that Alderson also worked at Ford. On Holland's widow's death in 1847 all was sold to the Turbutts of neighbouring Ogston, the house being let from 1855. The park seen here is now under Ogston Reservoir.

Glossop Hall

Set in a wooded park, Glossop Hall was built in 1850 around a more modest 17th century shooting lodge, originally called Royl Hall, to designs by Robert Abraham. Largely constructed of Millstone Grit sandstone with a slate roof, the house boasted a south front of 16 bays with a varying number of storeys set off by a round bell tower with a conical top. Inside were a magnificent carved oak ballroom fireplace of 1672 and a 'priest's hole', both of which survived from the previous house, built for the Earl of Shrewsbury. In 1616, the estate passed to the Duke of Norfolk, and his Howard descendants reduced and altered the house over the years.

Further alterations and additions were made by John Douglas of Chester at the beginning of the 20th century. The 9,110-acre estate was purchased in 1926 by Glossop Town Council and the house became Kingsmoor Residential School until 1953. It was finally demolished in 1956-7 and bungalows built on the site leaving no traces of the school or the former ice house. The park was re-named Manor Park and is Grade II in the National Register of Parks and Gardens.

Glapwell Hall

M. Craven, 1930s   *(2001)*

This substantial 2 and a half storey 7 bay house had 3 straight coped gables giving away its 17th century origin, and was taxed on 9 hearths in 1670. Mainly of coursed rubble Permian Magnesian Limestone, later harled, it stood on the ridge above the Doe Lea valley until demolished in 1957. An early 18th century range was added, east west, behind the 17th century front and more added on the north. In the 1870s a further wing was added on the west and a large conservatory to the north east. The Hallowes family inherited the estate from the Woolhouses and they from the Glapwells. The house was let to the Gorell-Barneses after World War I and sold after the Second World War, only the stables and summerhouse surviving.

Riber Castle (II), Matlock

M. Craven, postcard of c. 1904   *(2001)*

The gaunt ruins of the striking castellated house begun in 1861 for hydro magnate John Smedley (who was his own architect) and gutted nearly a century later, still remain on the ridge above Starkholmes, overlooking Matlock. Much of the accommodation lay between the towers and at its centre was a ballroom, the impressive glazed roof which was supported by painted and gilded Butterley Company ironwork.

Smedley's son sold the house to Rev. J. W. Chippet in 1888 who started a boys' school, which eventually closed in 1929. The chapel, seen here in about 1900, was originally the grandest and only domestic primitive Methodist chapel in the country.

The War Office used the house as a food store during World War Two and it was a school again after the war, but empty in the 1950s. It was gutted by the County Council in the late 1950s and taken over in 1962 as the Riber Fauna Reserve which closed in 1999. Plans are under review for its re-instatement as apartments amidst local opposition to the enabling development in the grounds. This a view of a former bedroom (then a dormitory), shows one of many marble fireplaces put in by Smedley. Here he used Italian marble.

Hopwell Hall (II)

Lt. Col. T. H. Pares, c.1910.   *(2001)*

Like Barrow Hall, fire prompted the demise of this early 18th century brick house, which was in consequence, demolished in 1957. It was built in 1720 for Henry Keyes, very much in the style of Francis Smith of Warwick. He had inherited its 16th century predecessor from the Sacheverells. Nottinghamshire County Council acquired the site in 1921 and after the fire replaced the house with new buildings.

Derby Museum, 1857   *(2001)*

Two storeys to go as demolition is well underway when this photograph was taken in 1957. A lodge and dovecote remain, but the replacement school has itself become redundant and has been privately acquired as a home. From 1734 to 1784 it was the seat of the Lakes Bts, and thereafter the Pares family.

Spondon Hall

M. Craven, 19th century lithograph by Moses Webster (2001)

Built for Roger Cox of Derby Shot tower fame in 1810, this brick and stucco Regency villa of 3 by 5 bays and 2 storeys was sold by the family to the Midland Railway and later LMS locomotive engineer Sir Henry Fowler, designer of the Royal Scot, died here in 1938. It was demolished in 1958 after 20 years of dereliction to make way for a local authority housing estate. Similar in style to The Pastures in Littleover, Derby, it was probably therefore designed by Alderman Richard Leaper. The park seen here was offered to the parish council in 1962 as public open space, but they refused and its fate was sealed.

Derby Evening Telegraph, 1957 (2001)

The house, faced from new in Derby-made Brookhouse's Roman Cement, was looking very dilapidated when this photograph was taken in the 1950s, probably just before demolition. It had been used by the army during World War Two, but no use found for it afterwards. The A52 bypass was punched through the park in 1964. The stable block with its stumpy brick tower echoed that at The Pastures in its mildly Gothic detailing.

Green Hall, Belper

J. Darwin, c.1900   *(2001)*

Built in 1809 for one of Jedediah Strutt's grandsons, also Jedediah, the hall replaced an earlier Green Hall, the appearance of which is unknown. The first Jedidiah Strutt's eldest son William, FRS, was the architect and he also designed bridges over Markeaton Brook and the fireproof calico mill in Derby as well as other family houses, for example Bridge Hill (see chapter 6). The family retained the house until 1930, but it had been tenanted since 1888. Used as an hospital in World War Two it was later divided into flats before being demolished in 1958.

Barrow Hall (III), Barrow on Trent

M. Craven, postcard of c.1904   *(2001)*

Another of Alderman Richard Leaper's brick and stucco houses, but this time built in 1809 for the Beaumonts. Slightly earlier than Spondon Hall, it fared no better as it was also demolished in 1958 after a disastrous fire. The garden front, seen here, was elegantly proportioned seven bays with two storeys and a pedimented breakfront embellished with a cartouche of the ancient and princely Beaumont arms.

The Beaumonts had settled at Barrow in the 1550s and finally the line became extinct in 1890, by which time the house had become the property (from 1881) of the Eadie family, Burton on Trent brewers. This view shows the bowed entrance front, which contained a flying cantilevered stone staircase with a cast iron balustrade, after the fire which broke out when the County Council owned house was unoccupied.

Ashbourne Hall (II)

Taxed on 10 hearths in 1670, making it Ashbourne's largest house, it was sold by Sir Aston Cokayne to the Boothbys the following year. Not long before 1772, when it was offered to let as "a convenient modern built mansion house", this ambitious stone house was probably extended and re-fronted in brick with 3 storeys and an east front of 4 bays which, with the 11 bay south front, is seen in this view taken in 1947.

A closer view of the south and east fronts in 1950, much of this was removed prior to 1960. Note that the irregular fenestration disguises earlier fabric. The present entrance still boasts an early Tudor ribbed vault.

M. Craven, postcard of 1905   *(2001)*

By 1901 the hall was an hotel, but by 1930 it was sold in lots and by 1948 was flats. The County Library and Freemasons have part of the south front, now without the top floor. The remaining three storey section was sold again in 2000 and refurbished by Mr and Mrs Cork. The large park, possibly by Emes, was split by the present Cokayne Avenue after the Great War and was partly built on and the rest dedicated as the War Memorial grounds and recreational park.

Measham Hall (II)

P. Withington, postcard of 1908   *(2001)*

Demolished in 1959, and built in 1767 for William Abney probably to designs by William Henderson of Loughborough. A pair of 2 storey pavilions, three bays over two arcaded ones topped with a pyramidal roof, were added a generation later. The house was sold by the Abneys in 1924 to the Measham Colliery Company for their manager's use, but in about 1946 was divided into flats. Mining subsidence later led to the inevitable demolition.

Spital House, Chesterfield

M. Craven, postcard of about 1914   *(1984)*

Probably originally a brick and timber-framed house, owned by the Earls of Shrewsbury from the Dissolution until 1616, it was clad in local Coal Measure Sandstone in the 17th century to become a typical 3 gabled 2 storey Derbyshire manor house. It was subsequently owned by various local families including the Woodyears, Bournes and Hunlokes, but it was probably the Bournes who added the odd-looking 18th century wing, part of which is visible on the extreme left of the view. Demolished in the 1950s after a period lying empty.

9

Houses destroyed
in the 1960s

Norbury Hall

M. Craven, postcard of c.1904 | (2001)

Designed by Giles and Brookhouse of Derby and built for S W Clowes in 1871–74 on land purchased from the Fitzherberts, latterly Lords Stafford, on the site of a former vicarage. It was of brick broadly banded in local Keuper Sandstone. This view of the (W) garden front fails to convey the rather large house behind. The grounds were laid out by William Barron and Son at the same time. The Hall was demolished as redundant in 1960.

Knowle Hill (II), Ticknall

M. Craven, 1985 | (2001)

The summerhouse range is a 5 bay Gothic brick house, attributable to Joseph Pickford for the Burdetts, and erected once Pickford finished building their seat at Foremark in 1761. It runs parallel with an earlier plain 6 bay timber-framed structure with 18th century brick nogging seen here. Both are single storey on the west where they face a much earlier house platform, and 2 storeys to the east where the land drops down into the upper part of a ravine. The house was completely abandoned in 1961, subsequently falling into ruin, but was restored by the Landmark Trust in 1990-93.

125

The original Francey's family manor house here was demolished around 1700 when Walter Burdett created a very odd house extending down the ravine, set in a landscape of his own contriving. His kinsman Sir Robert, Bt., lived there until Foremark was completed in 1761. The land northwards down to the Trent was then re-landscaped by William Emes in the Picturesque fashion and must be one of the earliest examples of this in the style region. Marris's drawing shows Pickford's range complete with its battlemented tower which collapsed prior to World War II, and of which little remains, although Emes' landscape survives under the wilderness.

At the top of the photograph is the entrance to an underground room, below the summerhouse range, flanked by niches and terraces perhaps for the accommodation of a convivial society where Sir Robert Burdett's friends, including Sir Francis Dashwood, made merry in the domed dining area behind. In the foreground are the excavated remains of the "curious house" built by Walter Burdett.

Darley Hall (II*), Darley Abbey

M. Craven, postcard of c.1930   *(2001)*

Francis Smith of Warwick built this house in 1723-5 for the noted local historian William Woolley. The brick 7 by 5 bay, 3 storey house was remodelled by Joseph Pickford in 1778 for Robert Holden, who had been fraudulently sold the estate by John Heath, a crooked Derby banker. The east front on this postcard view of c.1950 shows the 7 bays of the original house on either side by the Pickford additions covered in ivy.

Don Cook, 1960   *(2001)*

Pickford added beautifully proportioned but essentially plain ranges of 5 bays on the north and south fronts, the latter providing spectacular views down the Derwent to St. Helen's Park (which adjoined) and Derby. William Emes landscaped the spectacular park, which survives as a public open space. The Parapet was raised and the clock added in 1950.

Darley Abbey cotton miller Samuel Evans bought the estate in 1835, the family remaining there until the widow of the last Mr Evans gave the house and grounds to Derby Corporation in 1929. The park had been open to the public since the 1880s. The hall accomodated Derby Central School from the 1930s to 1958, after which it lay empty for four years before being unceremoniously and unnecessarily demolished in 1962. The fine late 19th century park gates by Edwin Haslam of Derby are seen in this view taken in 1970.

The house, as Derby Central School, showing the hall and fine oak staircase, quite possibly carved by Thomas Eborall of Warwick, Smith's usual joiner. Not visible is the ebonised wooden dial of a weather vane installed by John Whitehurst FRS in the 1760s, now in Derby Museum. Note the later decorative Minton tile floor so common in well-trodden areas.

Aldercar Park, Heanor (III)

M. Craven, postcard of July 1912 (2001)

Demolished in 1962 to make way for a new comprehensive school, this 4 bay 3 storey coursed rubble house had a substantial brick Arts and Crafts wing, almost Queen Anne Revival. It was added in the 1890s by Arthur Fitzherbert Wright, perhaps to designs by Naylor & Sale of Derby (a firm used elsewhere by the family), as the new entrance front.

M. Craven, postcard of c. 1900 (2001)

Thomas Burton built a house here in 1668 with a fine timber staircase. In the early 18th century the Milnes bought it but eventually sold to the Jessops, from whom it came to the Butterley Company. Under their ownership, it later became a preparatory school until purchased in 1898 by Fitzherbert Wright. Here the south front of the house is seen from the gardens.

Little Chester Manor (III), Derby

The late R. G. Hughes, 1964 *No entry*

This was one of three surviving Prebendal farms from the Reformation. When All Saints' College was founded in the 10th century, seven small estates were created in Little Chester to provide incomes for the Dean (later Sub-Dean) and the six canons. They were given to the Borough of Derby in 1554 and this one was held by the Bate family. Nathaniel Bate, the elder, built the pretty brick house c. 1610 directly on to the foundations of a Roman building of some pretension, suggesting long continuity on the site. After the death of his son Nathaniel, the estate reverted to the Corporation who let it as a farm until its demolition for Pickford & Co's garage in 1964.

Markeaton Hall (II), Derby

Derby Museum, 1950 *(2001)*

Sir John Mundy purchased the Markeaton estate in 1516 and built an ambitious high house taxed on 11 hearths in 1662 (see chapter 2). This was replaced by a bright red brick house by James Denstone for Wrightson Mundy in 1755. Joseph Pickford in 1772 added an orangery for his son, Francis, which survives, as does part of a twin courtyard stable block. William Emes, who lived on the estate at Bowbridge House, had previously landscaped the rather flat park with a lake, mill and cascade.

Francis Noel Clarke Mundy again extended the house in 1792, adding a new east entrance portico. It was later moved to the end of the West Walk as an eye catcher and replaced with a twin domed glass structure by Messenger & Co. of Loughborough and locally known as "Markeaton's Mae Wests", seen here.

Don Farnsworth, 1964 (2001)

Mrs Mundy gave the house to Derby Corporation in her will of 1929 "...for the purpose of an art gallery..." and her heir Revd. W G Clark-Maxwell later sold the 123 acre park to them. The Army commandeered the house in 1939 and it was demolished without ceremony in November 1964. (Yet another perfectly useable house demolished for dogmatic political reasons in a decade when socialist politicians sought to remove reminders of the "property owning classes".)

"Wouldn't it make a grand museum and art gallery?" Plenty of children visited the house, after the last war, using the building and its park for educational activities, as seen in this photograph from the collections of the now defunct Derbyshire Schools Museum Service that was housed across the park in Parkfield Cedars School building until the 1990s. Note also the two Handyside copies of the Warwick Vase subsequently also lost by a feckless City Council in the 1980s, along with the wrought iron orangery weather-vane made by Benjamin Yates.

Greenhill Hall (II), Norton

National Monument Record, 1960   *(2001)*

Originally built for the Bullock family in c.1560 in coursed rubble Coal Measure Sandstone of 2 storeys with 3 gables, the middle one lower and the outer ones with attics. Various local families owned the house until 1948 when Sheffield Corporation purchased the estate. Before demolition in 1964 a "Sheffield School" plaster ceiling from here was transferred to Cartledge Hall, but the extensive oak wainscotting and overmantels may also survive elsewhere too. Also discernible internally was a 3 bay timber framed hall house, probably 15th century or earlier.

Derby Museum, lithograph after George Bailey c. 1880   *(2001)*

A non-descript housing estate now covers the site and many country house estates purchased by local authorities suffered a similar fate. The Sheffield and Derby Corporations, in the 1960s, had a particularly awful record of demolition followed by poorly designed estates with mass housing of poor architectural quality. This 19th century drawing shows the "vegetative" style of allowing ivy and Virginia creeper and similar plants to climb over the stonework, a fashion prevalent from the Victorian and Edwardian periods right up to the 1960s although bad for the fabric of the house.

Sutton Rock, Sutton Scarsdale

Derby Museum 1923　　　　　　　　　　　　　　　　　　　　*No entry*

Described in the directories as "a beautiful residence a short distance from Sutton Hall", this substantial Italianate house, probably of Top Hard Rock from the estate, was built in 1848-1850 for Maj. William Arkwright (1809-1857) second son of Robert Arkwright of Sutton Scarsdale. William's brother Godfrey succeeded the latter for life, William's son remaining at Sutton Rock until succeeding to the estate in 1866. Thereafter it was the residence of the estate's agents, including Charles Cockburn (d. 1917) after whose time it was the home of Joscelyn Penrose, the Duke of Devonshire's agent. In 1946 he was succeeded by his son-in-law Hugo Read CBE and then in 1973 by his cousin, Derrick Penrose, recently High Sheriff. But the house itself was vacated around 1960, and demolished in advance of coal mining at the end of 1964.

Osmaston Manor (II)

M. Craven, postcard franked 1904　　　　　　　　　　　　　　　*(2001)*

Built for Francis Wright of the Butterley Company between 1846 and 1849 by H.I Stevens of Derby and one of the few Stevens houses that was demolished. Swanwick Hayes and extensions at Locko Park survive. In chunky Jacobean style, unusually in small coarse ashlar Carboniferous Limestone (from Kniveton) with Ashover Grit dressings (from Stanton), this striking large house of 2 and 3 storeys with towers had a 5 by 9 bay 2 storey cast iron conservatory, 80 feet in length, with a 5 light Romanesque window.

The house was heated by fires and under-floor pipes with smoke vented outside through pipes and flues, also under-floor, to a smoke tower in the kitchen garden. The interior was lavish; Derbyshire polished limestones, granites and Italian marble floors, oak everywhere and a 300 foot labour-saving railway in the cellars to carry coal to an hydraulic lift to all floors. Late in the century these innovations were replaced by conventional flues and chimneys. This photograph shows the castle-like towers and the additional chimneys.

The park included the rebuilt village of Osmaston, mostly by Stevens. House and estate were sold to Sir Andrew Barclay Walker 1st Bt. in 1884 who employed Sir Ernest George & Peto to enrich the interiors. The contents were sold separately. Sir Ian Walker removed to Okeover in 1962 and the house was demolished in 1965.

A view of the entrance hall, with its composite Serlian marble screen and the bottom pitch of the Imperial staircase. It is likely that some of the statuary seen here ended up in the Walker Art Gallery, Liverpool, founded by Sir Andrew Walker in 1877 and added to at his death in 1893. Certainly the giant deer (Irish Elk), the antlers of which are visible (shown left) ended up in Derby Museum.

A corner of the 100 acre park, showing the lake near the boathouse. The park and 36 acres of pleasure grounds were laid out by Edward Milner and "the famous Mr Pouty" with advice from Sir Joseph Paxton.

Parkfield Cedars, Derby

M. Craven, postcard of 1917 *No entry*

In the small hours of 6th February 1965 this fine brick and stucco suburban villa burnt out, forcing the girls' grammar school which had occupied it since 1917 eventually to re-locate. Indeed, the fire was providential for Derby Borough's plans for comprehensivisation. It had been built shortly before 1810 by amateur architect Alderman Richard Leaper for John Sandars, vintner, but was sold at his death in 1867 to the Wilmot-Sitwells of Stainsby House (see below). It was briefly a nursing home before becoming a school and acquiring considerable extensions, which remain. During the 1970s and 1980s it was home to the Derbyshire Museum Loan service to Schools.

Denby Old Hall (II*)

Private Collection, photograph by Richard Keene, c. 1875 *(2001)*

Coal open casting removed what was effectively two coursed rubble sandstone houses in 1966. The older house, concealed behind the trees in the photograph, was twin-gabled 16th century of 2 storeys and attics with a central 2 storey porch built for the Lowe family. The later portion of c.1630 with its front in line

with the wall of the older house, had the arms of Robey and Wilmot above the entrance. A Robey heiress married a Strelley in 1763 and from them it passed via heiresses to the Parker, Harris and Gregory families, each time reducing the estate by sales to bolster finances. It was bought back by the Lowes who, from 1884 became Drury-Lowes. The house declined into a tenanted farmstead surrounded by coal mines and was eventually divided up into cottages about 1950.

Pilsley Old Hall (II*)

RCHM(E), 1965

(1991)

A Grade II* listing should also have saved this mainly 17th century coarse ashlar local sandstone house from demolition, but on 13th August 1968 it ceased to exist. The original house, possibly 16th century and built for the Leake family, was doubled in size in the late 17th century by changing the entrance from north to south, keeping two gables along the increased length and inserting sashed windows on the new front as seen in the photograph. The porch is 19th century. The Leakes as Earls of Scarsdale sold in 1736 to the Caltons who sold in 1799 to Thomas Wilson. His heirs sold to the Sampsons and ultimately to F Gardner of Littleover who had it demolished.

Shallcross Hall, Whaley Bridge (II)

NMR, 1950

(2001)

Demolished in 1968, while in the ownership of ICI, the site of this pretty and unaltered early 18th century house standing on a ridge overlooking the Goyt Valley is now, inevitably, a housing estate. The coursed rubble Coal Measure Sandstone house of 1723-5 was built for John Shalcross, 15th in descent from the 13th century Swaine Shalcross, and reputedly by James Gibbs. However this is stylistically unlikely despite Gibbs's All Saints' Derby being built at precisely this time. It replaced another Shalcross family house taxed on 6 hearths in 1670 and probably early 17th century in date. Offices in the lower east end had stone remains of this previous house. (overleaf)

Private collection, 1935   *(2001)*

This view is of the parlour, to the left of the hall, which sports floor to ceiling 17th century panelling clearly visible together with the typically wide oak floor boards.

The drawing room showing wall panelling but only to dado height, all probably from the 17th century house. The estate passed to the Jacsons of Bebington in the 1730s, and was later acquired by the Fosters and then the Jodrells of Yeardsley before becoming the seat of the Halls from 1850. In 1926 Buxton Lime Firms acquired the freehold, later becoming ICI, who abandoned it for two decades before clearing it to extract limestone, later selling the utterly transformed site to the local authority.

The fine hall screen is chunky enough to be reminiscent of the circle of Sir John Vanburgh. Did the architect use an old pattern book? The detailing was of high quality throughout, suggesting a local builder/architect of some flair was responsible.

Alfreton Hall (II)

Francis Smith of Warwick built this ashlared Coal Measure Sandstone house in 1724-26 for the Morewoods when he was building All Saints', Derby for James Gibbs. The Morewoods' earlier house, taxed on 16 hearths, was built nearer the church on the site of the later Hall Farm. Inside there was a fine wooden staircase, rococo stuccowork and in 1796 an inlaid marble section of strata across Derbyshire by White Watson of Bakewell was installed. That same year the Morewoods died out. Their heirs-by-marriage, the Palmer-Morewoods, enlarged the house by two 5 bay wings of 2 storeys and a tetrastyle ionic portico as seen in the photograph.

The house was again extended in 1855 by the addition of an east wing to designs by Benjamin Wilson of Alfreton (later of Derby). This today is all that remains, as the 18th century house, seen here from the south, was demolished in 1968 by its then owners, the Local Authority, as it had become weakened by mining subsidence.

Breadsall Mount

The late R. G. Hughes, 1967 colour slide   *(2001)*

In between "restoring" Derbyshire churches, H. I Stevens of Derby and his partner Frederick Josias Robinson, built this largish Victorian house of 2 storeys and attics in the local Rough Rock for Thomas Osbourne Bateman in 1863. An attached lower service wing with a loggia and a separate classical stable block completed the buildings.

The late R. G. Hughes, 1967   *(2001)*

The Batemans sold in 1929 and the house became the Bishop of Derby's palace until 1968 when Derby Corporation bought it before demolishing it. The small park, on the ridge, is now St Andrew's View connecting Breadsall and Chaddesden with a school and housing. The photograph shows the arms of Dr Courtney Pearce, the first Bishop of Derby, impaled by the Derby diocese proudly fixed above the main entrance.

Temple House, Derby

M. Craven, photograph from a Borough publication, 1930s   *No entry*

A particularly interesting villa of c. 1820 in Keuper sandstone attributable to Alderman Richard Leaper (1759-1838), although the client's name is unclear. The name perhaps suggests a pioneer of Derby's Tyrian Freemasonic Lodge, founded in 1794, and it may have been for Joseph Woollat, a relative of the Strutts. It was typically eccentric, and sported the architect's favourite sliding cast iron jalousies, made by the local firm of Weatherhead, Glover & Co. It was, however, for most of the Victorian era, home to John Bailey, JP (married to Wollatt's widow), long the chairman of the Derby bench and a rich businessman. It later had a variety of institutional uses, latterly in Borough ownership and was cleared to make way for a clinic.

10
Houses destroyed since 1970

Heanor Old Hall

Heanor Local History Soc, c.1950 (2001)

Demolished in 1972, this early 18th century brick farmhouse was probably built over the core of the original timber-framed house of 1550 of the Roper family. Latterly almost always tenanted, it was divided into miners' cottages and eventually succumbed to re-development.

Kirk Hallam Hall

Derby Museum, drawing of c.1890 No entry

For much of the middle Ages the Greys of Codnor held Kirk Hallam, but from 1562 to 1736 the Leakes of Sutton Scarsdale had it. When the 4th Earl of Scarsdale died the Newdigates bought it and built a Georgian house next to the church. After rebuilding in the Regency period, it was tenanted by Joseph Prince, later William Adlington and by the 1890s Francis Darwin Huish, a Derby solicitor, was living in the house as seen in the drawing of about that time. In 1932 it became a vicarage, being shorn of its estate, reduced and rebuilt accordingly. It was demolished by the Church in 1973 to be replaced by a "purpose built" vicarage.

Whittington Manor (II)

DLC, 1960s

(2001)

This typical late 16th century stone slate roofed, L-shaped, coursed rubble house with 17th century additions was deceptively large. The cranked hood moulds, mullioned windows and the two-storey porch are prominent and behind was a two-storey stair tower. Demolished in 1970 after a lengthy period of dereliction, this important house made way for a modern bungalow bearing the datestone 1977, a great loss.

M. Craven, 1960s

(2001)

The Whittington family had a house here in the 12th century, thereafter passing through the centuries to the Dethicks and Poles, and by sale to the Friths, Gillets, Dixons, Fowlers and ending up with the Claytons by 1900. Various tenants followed, but by 1969 listed building consent to demolish finally sealed its fate. Note the 2 door "modern" conveniences in the front garden – handy for the night soil collectors!

Holme Hall, Newbold-with-Dunston

Chesterfield Library, photograph of c. 1960   *No entry*

An important 1970s loss, little remarked at the time, was the last vestige of the Hall on the important manorial estate of Holme. Before 1483, the heiress of Robert Whittington (and of his nephew Henry Bakewell of Holme) married Roger, 4th son of Sir Robert Eyre of Padley, and much of the estate remained in Eyre hands until 1835, although they retained ownership of the surviving Newbold chapel much longer. However, the hall itself was sold to the Leakes in 1595 and was reduced progressively until this vaguely *cottage orne* farmhouse remained, built in the late Regency for J. H. Barker, of Coal Measure Sandstone. It was said to contain the vestiges of the timber-framed great hall of the Eyres' seat, although an extant nearby pub also claims to be a fragment of the house.

Stainsby House, Smalley (II)

RCHM(E), 1967   *(2001)*

The early history of this rambling, largely ashlared, classical house is obfuscated by complexity but an early 18th century villa, purchased by John Fletcher (d.1734) from the Moor family (having been held much earlier by the de Steynesbys), was re-modelled by Thomas Gardner in about 1780 for Fletcher's daughter Elizabeth. She had married Francis Barber of Greasley, Nottinghamshire, but her son sold the estate, and within a few years it was in the hands of Edward Sacheverell Wilmot, of the Chaddesden family and heir of William Sacheverell of Morley. This view shows the entrance front and the east range extension.

Wilmot acquired most of Morley, adjoining the Stainsby estate, through descent and his increased lands prompted a building extension on the north-west. Edward Degge Wilmot-Sitwell, his son, added the east range in 1837 and linked the wings of the entrance with the loggia. His nephew Robert glassed it in about 1900. The photograph shows a detail of the main entrance on the south front.

The Wilmot-Sitwells eventually sold to a poultry farmer, but the house became a Roman Catholic school for a while before being demolished in 1972 to make way for an extraordinary new house by David Shelley of Nottingham for R Morley. The gardens laid out by William Barron and Sons in 1914 survive. Also of note in this view of the main staircase is the remarkable thickness of the main north-south wall and the 4 thick stumpy Doric column supports, both of which point to efforts to counter to coal mining subsidence.

The drawing room survived unaltered from Gardner's alterations of c.1780. Note the carved fire surround and plaster overmantel with inset portrait frame and fruit and game pendants in the style of Grinling Gibbons.

This striking 5 bay pavilion to the west of the main house was perhaps John Fletcher's early 18th century villa, modified during the Regency period to lend unity with the main house, of which it was used as part of the service accommodation.

Betty Hughes, a local artist and wife of the late Roy Hughes, for many years Deputy Curator of Derby Museum, drew this view of the monumental and asymmetrical south front during the house's decline.

Oakhurst, Ambergate

M. Craven, from a postcard of c. 1924   *No entry*

Oak Hurst is older than it looks, having started out in 1848 as Forge House and leased out by the Hurts, with their ironworks alongside, to John & Charles Mold, bankrupt in 1865. In 1888 it was enlarged for the Midland Railway, probably by their architect Charles Trubshaw, for Richard Bird, the superintendent engineer.

M. Craven, postcard of c. 1900   *No entry*

About 1893 it was acquired by Mancunian John Thewlis Johnson, who adapted the old forge into a wire works, and in 1894 the house took its present form as neo-Jacobean Arts and Crafts built in Ashover Grit sandstone and timber framing, the architect probably being John Douglas of Chester. In 1924 it was dedicated as a Diocesan Retreat House, but after military occupation was converted for flats in 1945. By the 1970s it was empty, and has decayed ever since being now ruinous and likely to be cleared at any time.

Potlock House, Findern (II)

M. Craven, photograph of August 1981   *No entry*

The ancient manor house of Potlock passed from the de Potlocks to the Willingtons and the Tokes, who had a chapel here. It then passed via the Findernes to the Harpurs, under whom it was reduced and tenanted as a farm. The last vestiges of the old manor were reputedly cleared in 1805 by John Glover, who replaced it with this stuccoed brick house of some charm, which, from the irregularity of its fenestration, probably contained elements of its predecessor. The proximity of Willington Power station and the advance of gravel extraction caused it to be vacated in 1981 and demolished a year later. Scandalously, the site still has not been quarried, the *raison d'etre* for the demolition in the first place.

Stuffynwood Hall, Shirebrook

DCC, 1960   *(1984)*

Built of rock-faced Permian Magnesian Limestone in an odd, almost "haunted house" style, in 1858 from a pre-existing farmhouse, for Robert Malkin. It was purchased and considerably enlarged by Joseph Paget in 1873 who also landscaped the park a year later. In 1915 it was sold to the Markhams, iron founders of Chesterfield, but was unoccupied by 1925, used by the military during World War Two and demolished in 1988. This photograph shows the SW portion of the house after demolition of the big, ugly pyramidally-topped tower that joined the two main ranges, that beyond having been lower and simpler in design.

Burnaston House, Etwall (II)

J. Darwin, photo by Richard Keene, 1860   *(1991)*

An ashlar faced Keuper Sandstone villa built in 1824 in the "stripped" classical style of Sir John Soane by Samuel Brown of Derby for A. N. E. Mosley (1792-1875) who had acquired the preceding house, Conygree Hall, of which no illustrations survive. This view of Burnaston by Richard Keene shows the south front in 1860.

M. Craven, March 1990   *(1991)*

It was purchased from Col. Godfrey Mosley (who had succeeded to Calke Abbey) by Derby Borough Council in 1936 and it acted as Derby Airport clubhouse and terminal until 1968 when East Midlands Airport opened. It then declined to dereliction before being bought by J. Keck in 1987 as an old people's home and it was half restored (with a vast EH grant) when compulsorily purchased for immediate demolition to make way for the Toyota car

plant. Thereupon Kevin Ellis, of Gainsborough Properties, carefully dismantled the house stone by stone and palletted it. Here the south front awaits removal.

Several schemes to re-build the house fell through due to obdurate objectors and the fabric on its pallets still awaits a site. Samples of interior detailing – plasterwork, stair balusters, etc. – were rescued by a local expert, from which copies could be re-worked. Burnaston is a sad tale of vested interests, political pressure on local authorities, and gross NIMBYism. Even the stables (latterly a residence and completely demolished) have a sad expression!

Willington House

Alan Gifford, postcard of 1900   *No entry*

This began life, probably in the 18th century, as a substantial farmhouse on the estate of the Spilsbury family. On the death of Revd. Francis Ward Spilsbury it came to Francis Barber of Etwall Lodge, who doubled it in size, but in different proportions, in order to produce two reception rooms with suitably high ceilings. In 1875 it was let to George S. Messiter, who ran it as a "Gentlemen's Preparatory School". Attractive gardens laid out by Barrons for the Leys stretched down to the banks of the Trent.

When the school closed in 1899 it was sold to Sir Francis Ley, 1ˢᵗ Bt., a Derby ironfounder, who installed his son H. Gordon Ley who later added a gabled cross- wing. Between the wars, it was occupied by Ley's manager Ian Forbes Panton, and by his widow. In the 1950s it was sold as an hotel. This closed in December 2000 and the house was demolished in October 2001 to make way for a housing development.

Bibliography & Resource List

A list of books and other sources that were used in the preparation of 'Lost Houses of Derbyshire' and / or will be of use to those seeking to delve further into the county's history.

ABERG, F. A., (Ed.) Medieval Moated Sites, CBA Research Report No. 17 (London, 1978)

ADAM, W., The Gem of the Peak (Derby, 1840)

ADAMS, N., A History of Walton-on-Trent (Walton, 2000)

AIKIN, J., A Description of the Country from Thirty to Forty Miles Round Manchester (London, 1795)

AIRS, M., The Tudor & Jacobean Country House – A Building History (Godalming, 1998)

AITKEN, M., et al., Smalley Remembered (Heanor, 1990)

AITKENHEAD, N., and STEVENSON, I. P., Geology of the country around Buxton, Leek and Bakewell. (London HMSO, 1985) Mem.Br.Geol.Surv.

ANCIENT MONUMENT SOCIETY Journal (Since 1956)

ANDREWS, M., Long Ago in Peakland (Nottingham, 1948)

ANON, The History and Topography of Ashbourne and the Valley of the Dove (Ashbourne, 1839)

ARCHITECTURAL HISTORY Journal of the Society of Architectural Historians (London, from 1957)

ARKELL, W. J., Oxford Stone (London, 1947)

ARMITAGE, H., Chantry Land (London, 1910)

BAGSHAW, S., Directory of Derbyshire (Derby, 1846)

BARLEY, M., The English Farmhouse and Cottage (London, 1961)

BARRON, W., The British Winter Garden (London, 1852)

BARRON & SON LTD., A List of some of the Principal Works (Derby, n.d. [c.1929])

BARRY, C. et al, Report of the Commissioners on the Selection of Stone for the New Houses of Parliament (London, 1839)

BATEMAN, C., A Descriptive and Historical Account of Alfreton (Derby, 1812)

BEARD, G., Craftsmen and Interior Decoration in England 1660-1820 (London, 1981)

BEARD, G., Decorative Plasterwork in Great Britain (London, 1975)

BEARD, G., The Work of Robert Adam (London, 1978)

BENNETT, J. D., The Vanished Houses of Leicestershire, (Leicester, 1971)

BESTALL, J. M. (Ed. Fowkes, D.V.), A History of Chesterfield, Vol III (Chesterfield, 1978)

BIGSBY, R., Historical and Topographical Description of Repton (London, 1854)

BLORE, T., A History of the Manor…of South Wingfield 2 Vols. (London, 1793)

BOWYER, L. J., The Ancient Parish of Norbury (Ashbourne, 1953)

BOYES, M., Allestree Hall (Derby, 1982)

BRIGGS, J. J., History of Melbourne, (2nd edn., Derby, 1846)

BRISCOE, J. P., Nottinghamshire and Derbyshire at the Beginning of the Twentieth Century (Brighton, Briscoe 1901)

BRITTON, J. & BRAYLEY, E. W., The Beauties of England & Wales Vol. III (London 1802)

BRUNSKILL, R. W., Illustrated Handbook of Vernacular Architecture (London, 1971)

BRUNSKILL, R. W., Brick Building in Britain (London, 1990)

BULMER, T., Directory of Derbyshire (London, 1895)

BURKE, J. B., Visitation of Seats…of the Noblemen and Gentlemen of Great Britain & Ireland (2 Vols. London, 1852-3)

BURKE, J. B., Visitation of Seats…(Second series, 2 Vols. London, 1854-5)

BURTON, I. E., The Royal Forest of the Peak (Bakewell, 1967)

CHISHOLM, J.I., et al Geology of the country around Ashbourne and Cheadle (London, HMSO 1988)

CHOLERTON, P., Chaddesden (Stroud, 1999)

CHRISTIAN, R. C., Derbyshire (London, 1978)

CLAY, R. M., Samuel Hieronymus Grimm of Burgdorf in Switzerland (London, 1939)

CLIFTON-TAYLOR, A., The Pattern of English Building (London, 1972)

CLIFTON-TAYLOR, A. & IRESON, A. S., English Stone Building (London, 1983)

COLVIN, Sir H. M., Biographical Dictionary of British Architects (3rd edn. London, 1995)

COLVIN, Sir H. M., Calke Abbey (London, 1985)

COLVIN, Sir H. M., The Country Seat (London, 1970)

COULSON, C. L. H., A Handlist of English Royal Licences to Crenellate 1200-1578 (Unpublished MS 1982)

COUNTRY LIFE (London, from 1897)

CRAVEN, M. A. J. B., Richard Keene's Derby (Derby, 1993)

CRAVEN, M. A. J. B., The Derby Town House (Derby, 1987)

CRAVEN, M. A J. B., The Illustrated History of Derby's Suburbs (Derby, 1996b)

CRAVEN, M. A. J. B., & STANLEY, M. F., The Derbyshire Country House 2 Vols (Matlock, 1982, 1984)

CRAVEN, M. A. J. B., & STANLEY, M. F., The Derbyshire Country House New & Rev Edn. (Derby, 1991)

CROFTS, J., & READ. J., Footsteps Through Smalley (Smalley, 1995)

CUTTS, C. G., History of Thornbridge Hall (Ashford, 1986)

DAVIES, D. P., A View of Derbyshire (Belper, 1811)

DERBY COUNTY BOROUGH COUNCIL Official Opening of the Municipal Airport, Programme 7 June 1939 (Derby, 1939)

DURANT, D. N., Bess of Hardwick (London, 1977)

DURANT, D. N. & RIDEN, P. (Eds.), The Building of Hardwick Hall Pt. I, (DRS IV, Chesterfield, 1980)

DURANT, D. N. & RIDEN, P. (Eds.), The Building of Hardwick Hall Pt. II, (DRS IX, Chesterfield, 1984)

EDEN, R. A., et al, The Geology of the Country Around Sheffield (London, 1957)

EDWARDS, D. G. (Ed.), Derbyshire Hearth Tax Assessments 1662-1670 (DRS VII Chesterfield, 1982)

EDWARDS, D. G., The Hunlokes of Wingerworth Hall 2nd Edn. (Wingerworth, 1976)

EGGLESHAW, P., et al., Around Old Heanor (Heanor, 1982)

EMERY, A., The Greater Medieval Houses of England & Wales Vol. 2 (Cambridge, 2000)

FAREY, J., A General View of the Agriculture and Minerals of Derbyshire 3 Vols. (London, 1811)

FEARNEYHOUGH, H. W., Chaddesden – A History (Derby, 1991)

FELLOWS, R. A., Sir Reginald Blomfield (London, 1985)

FERREY, E. B., South Wingfield Manor (London, 1876)

FITTON, R. S. & WADSWORTH, A. P., The Strutts and the Arkwrights 1758-1830 (Manchester, 1958)

FLEMING, L. & GORE, A., The English Garden (London, 1979)

FLETCHER, S. B., The Fletcher House of Lace (Derby, 1957)

FORD, T., A History of Chesterfield (Chesterfield, 1839)

FRANKLYN, J., The Gentleman's Country House and its Plan, 1835-1914 (London, 1981)

FRASER, W., The Parishes of Swarkstone and Stanton-by-Bridge (Burton-on-Trent, 1944)

FRITH, J. B., Highways and Byways in Derbyshire (London, 1920)

FROST, D. & SMART, J. G. O., Geology of the Country North of Derby (London, 1979)

GEORGIAN GROUP Journal (London, from 1990)

GIBBS, J., Book of Architecture (London, 1728)

GIBSON, W. et al, Geology of the Southern Part of the Derbyshire and. Nottinghamshire Coalfield (London, 1908)

GIBSON, W. & WEDD, C. B., Geology of the Northern Part of the Derbyshire Coalfield (London, 1913)

GIROUARD, M., Robert Smythson and the Elizabethan Country House (2nd Edn. London, 1983)

GIROUARD, M., The Victorian Country House (London, 1979)

GLOVER, S., Directory of Derbyshire (Derby, 1827-9)

GLOVER, S., History and Gazetteer of the County of Derby, 2 Vols. (1st Edn. Derby 1829/31; 2nd. Edn. Derby 1831/33)

GLOVER, S., Notes on the History of Derbyshire (Derby,1842)

GLOVER, S., The Peak Guide (Derby, 1830)

GOMME, A., The Genesis of Sutton Scarsdale in Colvin, Sir H. M., The Country Seat (London, 1970)

GOMME, A., Francis Smith of Warwick (Donnington, 2001)

GOW, I & RONAN, A., The Scottish Country House (Edinburgh 1995)

GREEN, A. H. et al, Geology of the Carboniferous Limestone, Yoredale Rocks and Millstone Grit of North Derbyshire (London, 1887)

HALL, S. T., Days in Derbyshire (Derby 1863)

HARRIS, J., The Artist and the Country House (London, 1979)

HARRIS, J., The Design of the English Country House 1620-1920 (London, 1985)

HARRIS, J., No Voice from the Hall: Early Memories of a Country House Snooper (London, 1998)

HART, C., North Derbyshire Archaeological Survey (Chesterfield, 1981)

HASLAM, C., Knowle Hill, An Interim Report (Shottesbrooke, 1993)

HENDERSON, J. B. & ROBINSON, E. R., The Etwall Heritage (Ilkeston, 1979)

HENSTOCK, A. et al., A Georgian Town, Ashbourne 1725-1825 2 Vols. (Ashbourne, 1989, 1991)

HENSTOCK, A. et al., Victorian Town (Ashbourne, 1978)

HERRMANN, L., Paul and Thomas Sandby (London, 1986)

HEWETT, C. A., English Historic Carpentry (Chichester, 1980)

HILL, O & CORNFORTH, J., English Country Houses, Caroline 1625-1685 (London, 1966)

HIPKINS, F. C., Repton and its Neighbourhood (Repton, 1899)

HOLDEN, W., The Derbyshire Holdens and Their Descendants (London, 1930)

HOLME, C., The Gardens of England in the Midland and Northern Counties (London, 1908)

HOLMES, M. , The Country House Described (London, 1986)

HOSKINS, W. C., The Making of the English Landscape (London, 1955)

HOWARD, M., The Early Tudor Country House (London, 1987)

HULL, E., Building and Ornamental Stones (London, 1872)

HULL, E., The Triassic and Permian Rocks of the Midland Counties of England (London, 1869)

HUNT, B. J., West Hallam Heritage (Ilkeston, 1978)

HUNTER, J. Pedigrees (Harleian Society, Vol. LXXXVIII, London, 1936)

HUNTER, J., South Yorkshire (London, 1828)

HUSSEY, C., English Country Houses, Mid-Georgian (London, 1956)

HUTTON, B et al., Derby Buildings Records (Derbys. Archaeological Society Architectural Group)

HUTTON, B., Historic Farmhouses Around Derby (Cromford, 1991)

HUTTON, W., History of Derby to the Year 1791 (London, 1791)

IBBETSON, P., The Gardens of Shipley Hall (Matlock, 1986)

JACQUES, A. S., Melbourne (Derby, 1933)

JACQUES, D., Georgian Gardens: the Reign of Nature (London, 1983)

JENNINGS, J. R. G. et al., Belper (Belper, 1981)

JOHNSON, R., A History of Alfreton (Ripley, 1968)

KELLY'S Directories of Derbyshire (London, 1877, 1891, 1903/8/12/ 25/28/32/36/41)

KERRY, Rev. C., History and Legends of Smalley (Derby, 1905)

KETTLE, P., Oldcotes (Cardiff, 2000)

KETTLE, P., The Sutton Scarsdale Story (Chesterfield, 1988)

KIP, J., Nouveau Theatre de Grande Bretagne Vol. I (London, 1715)

LEES-MILNE, J., English Country Houses, Baroque 1685-1715 (London, 1970)

LELAND, J., Itinerary of a Tour Through England and Wales, Leland 1545 (Oxford, 1710)

LUCAS, R., The Manor of Markeaton, Mackworth & Allestree 1650-1851 (Derby, 1995)

LUGARD, C. E., The Saints and Sinners of Ashover (Leicester, 1924)

LYSONS, S. & D., Magna Britannia, Vol. V., (London 1816)

MADAN, F. C., The Gresleys of Drakelow (London, 1899)

MERCER, E., English Vernacular Houses (London, 1975)

MEREDITH, R., Farms and Families of Hathersage Outseats (2 parts, Rotherham, 1981,1983)

MOORE, A., A Son of the Rectory (Gloucester, 1982)

MOORE, P., The End of an Era (Snelston, 2000)

MORLEY Village History Committee, History of the Parish of Morley (Ilkeston, 1977)

MORRIS, C., (Ed.) The Journeys of Celia Fiennes (London, 1949)

MORRIS, F. 0. (Ed.), A Series of Picturesque Views of the Country Seats of Great Britain &.Ireland 6 Vols. (London, 1880)

MORROW, E., Willington Memories (Lancaster, n.d.)

MOWL, T., & EARNSHAW, B., Trumpet at a Distant Gate (London, 1985)

NEALE, J. P., Views of Seats…6 Vols. (London, 1818-23)

NICHOLS, J., The History and Antiquities of the County of Leicester, 4 Vols. In 8 (London, 1795-1811)

PAYNE, C. J., Derby Churches Old & New or, Derby's Golgotha (Derby, 1893)

PEVSNER, Sir N., Buildings of England
  Cheshire (London, 1971)
  Derbyshire (London, 1953)
  Leicestershire, (London, 1970)
  Yorkshire, West Riding (London, 1967)

PILKINGTON, J., A View of the Present State of Derbyshire, 2 Vols., (Derby, 1789)

REEDMAN, K., The Book of Long Eaton (Buckingham, 1979)

REEDMAN. K. et al., Around Old Heanor (Heanor, 1981)

REID, P., County List of Houses Destroyed in Great Britain and Ireland, Vol. 1 (1981)

RELIQUARY, The, Ed. Ll. Jewitt (Derby, 1860-92)

ROBERTSON, C. L., Historical Rooms from the Manor houses of England 2 Vols. (London, 1929)

RYAN, S. D. M., A Short History of Foremark (London, 1965)

SAUNDERS, E. J., Joseph Pickford of Derby (Stroud, 1993)

SCOTT, J., SMITH, J. H., & WINTERBOTTOM, D., Glossop Dale, Manor & Borough (Glossop, 1986)

SHAW, S., The History and Antiquities of Staffordshire, 2Vols. (London, 1798, 1801)

SITWELL, Sir R. S., Bt., Renishaw Hall & the Sitwells (Derby, 1985)

SLATER, J. Directory of Derbyshire (1862)

SMITH, E. G. et al, Geology of the Country Around Chesterfield, Matlock and Mansfield, (London, 1967)

STANLEY, M. F., The Stone Slates of Derbyshire, (forthcoming)

STANLEY, M. F. The Building Stones of Dale Abbey. Report to Derbys. County Council for Dale Abbey Conservation Area (unpublished, 1977)

STANLEY, M.F. Carved in Bright Stone. In Parsons, D. (ed) Stone quarrying and building in England AD43-1525 (Chichester, 1990)

STRONG, Sir R., BINNEY, M. & HARRIS, J. The Destruction of the Country House (London, 1974)

THOMPSON, M., The Construction of the Manor at South Wingfield, Derbyshire in Siveking, G., (Ed.) Problems in Social and Economic Archaeology Part IV (London, 1976)

THOROLD, H. C., The Shell Guide to Derbyshire (London, 1972)

THOROTON, R., History of Nottinghamshire, Ed. Throsby, J. with additions, 3 Vols. (London, 1797)

THORPE, F. S., The Heritage of Loscoe & Codnor (Loscoe, 1990)

TILLEY, J., The Old Halls, Manors and Families of Derbyshire, 4 Vols., (Derby, 1892-1902)

TIPPING, H. A., English Homes, Period 6, Vol. I (London, 1926)

TIPPING, H. A., Gardens Old and New 3 Vols. (London, n.d. [c.1908])

TURBUTT, G., A History of Ogston (Ogston, 1975)

TURBUTT, G., A History of Derbyshire 4 Vols. (Cardiff, 1999)

USHER, H., Castles in the Air (Derby, 1997)

USHER, H., Knowle Hill 2nd, Rev.Edn. (Ticknall, 1993)

USHER, H., The Hardinges of King's Newton (Derby, 1996)

VICTORIA HISTORY OF THE COUNTIES OF ENGLAND. Derbyshire, 2 Vols. (London, 1905)

WAIN, H., A Brief History of Bretby (1964)

WATSON, J., British and Foreign Building Stones (Cambridge, 1911)

WATSON, S., A History of Mickleover and Littleover (Derby, 1993)

WATSON, S., Spondon – A History (Spondon, 1989)

WATSON, W, The Strata of Derbyshire (Sheffield, 1811)

WHITE, T., Gazeteer of the County of Derby, (London, 1857)

WILSON, M. I., The Country House and its Furnishings (London, 1977)

WOLFE, J. & GANDON, J., Vitruvius Britannicus Vol. V (London, 1771)

WOOD, M., The English Medieval House (London, 1965)

WOOLLEY, W., History of Derbyshire Ed. Glover, C & Riden, P. DRS VI (Chesterfield, 1981)

YOULGREAVE WOMENS' INSTITUTE, Some Account of Youlgreave Middleton and Alport, (Bakewell, 1931)

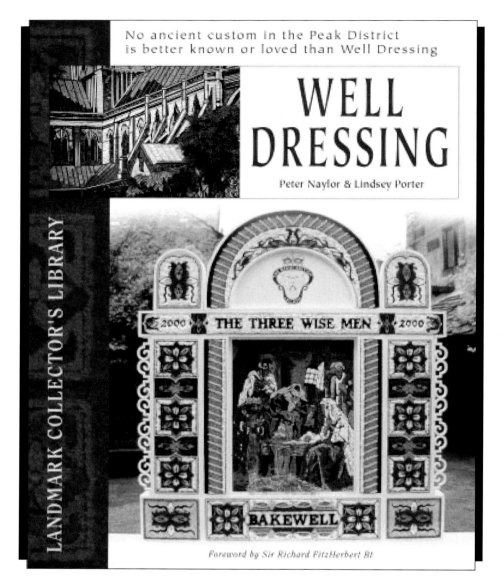

No ancient custom in the Peak District is better known or loved than Well Dressing

WELL DRESSING

Peter Naylor & Lindsey Porter

THE THREE WISE MEN

2000   2000

BAKEWELL

Foreword by Sir Richard FitzHerbert Bt

LANDMARK COLLECTOR'S LIBRARY

Well Dressing
Peter Naylor & Lindsey Porter
ISBN: 1 84306 023 X

128pp, 150 full colour photographs, with drawings and early black and white photographs. High quality paper. 276mm x 219mm. Hardback with laminated wipe-clean dust jacket £19.95

This important new book is the first hardback history of Well Dressing. By the end of the 18th century, the custom in Derbyshire was virually extinct: only Tissington carried on the practice. It was, however, revived as a celebration of the introduction of piped water. Now many villages have adapted the custom, often reviving it after a lapse of many decades. Peter Naylor and Lindsey Porter have brought together the history of well dressing both within and beyond Derbyshire. The book includes a list of villages known to have dressed wells and a detailed account of the well dressing process. In addition to some old drawings of dressed wells and some early black and white photographs, this beautifully illustrated book has over 70 colour photographs of dressed wells and 70 more of the ancient art and more modern techniques of well dressing.

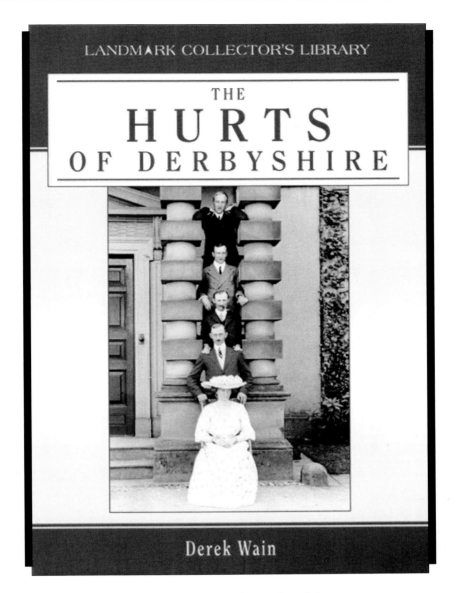

The Hurts of Derbyshire
Derek Wain
ISBN: 1-84306-042-6

192pp hardback £24-95

The Hurt family can trace their origins back to 1489 when they were resident at Green Hall, Ashbourne, Derbyshire. In 1617 they purchased Casterne Hall in the nearby Manifold Valley. The family eventually settled at Alderwasley Hall near the River Derwent in the southern Peak District.

The family remained at Alderwasley until the 1930's when the hall and its contents were sold, but to this day the family live at Casterne Hall. This book recalls the known history of each generation since 1648. Almost all of the family since 1860 (including Francis Hurt, 1803 - 1862) have been photographed, creating a unique portfolio of family images which stretches back 200 years. Most of these were taken by Alice Hurt and many of her early views around the district are published for the first time.

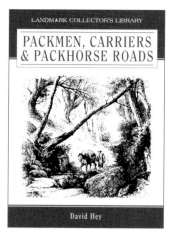
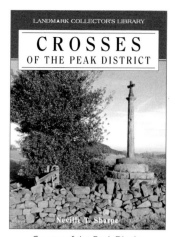
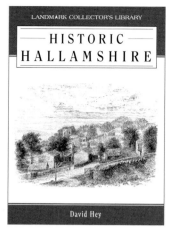
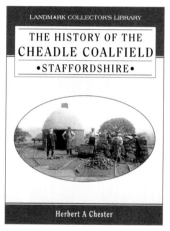
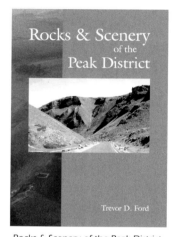
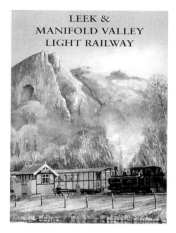